From the
Darkness
to the
Light

*My Journey
with the Masters*

Rev. Paul Kwame Kyei

DARJEELING PRESS
Emigrant, Montana

*I dedicate this book to
my Guru, Elizabeth Clare Prophet,
without whose love the Path
would have been lost to me
in this life.*

FROM THE DARKNESS TO THE LIGHT
My Journey with the Masters
by Rev. Paul Kwame Kyei
Copyright © 2012 Darjeeling Press
All rights reserved

For information, contact
Darjeeling Press
PO Box 154, Emigrant, MT 59027 USA
www.darjeelingpress.com

ISBN: 978-1-937217-06-8 (softbound)
ISBN: 978-1-937217-07-5 (eBook)

Maps adapted from originals courtesy
United Nations Cartographic Section

Special thanks to The Summit Lighthouse for
permission to include the following material in this book:
"Decree to Helios and Vesta," "Salutation to the Sun," "Traveling
Protection," "Heart, Head and Hand Decrees," "Lord Michael, Cut Me
Free!" "Reverse the Tide," "Decree to Beloved Mighty Astrea," and "I AM
the Violet Flame" from *Prayers, Meditations and Dynamic Decrees for
Personal and World Transformation,* published by The Summit Lighthouse,
© 1984, 2010; *Your Opportunity to Become the Christ (Christ in the
Threefold Flame),* Ascended Master Afra, and photographs of
Elizabeth Clare Prophet © Summit Publications, Inc.

For more information about The Summit Lighthouse,
Church Universal and Triumphant or the
Teachings of the Ascended Masters, contact
The Summit Lighthouse
63 Summit Way, Gardiner, MT 59030 USA
1-800-245-5445 • +1 406 848 9500
www.TSL.org
tslinfo@TSL.org

Contents

Preface

Life is a complex adventure.

The holy scriptures say that we are saved to serve. It is not a question of just being saved, but rather being saved for a purpose—and that purpose is to serve. We are still here because we have to finish our work.

Every moment we find ourselves in this octave is a dispensation given to us so that we can draw closer to fulfilling the expectation of light. And so we do not serve begrudgingly, but we fulfill our service with joy, knowing full well that one day, sooner or later, we will be called home.

Do we go home smiling broadly because of a work well done?

Or do we go home grumbling because of opportunities not taken and a failed mission? God forbid.

The choice is before us each day.

My own journey began in a village in Ghana, in West Africa. My father was a fetish priest, a practitioner of our traditional religion. As a boy, I became a Christian, the first in my family. I served in the Methodist Church for many years, and I was known there as a fiery preacher.

Then I found the ascended masters, the great souls of East and West, from all races and religions, who have ascended back to God, as Jesus did. In every age, these masters have sent messengers and prophets to deliver their teachings to the world.

Elizabeth Clare Prophet, one of these messengers, became my teacher.

I have followed the path of the ascended masters and their teachings for nearly forty years. In those years I have witnessed miracles and passed through many tests and challenges. I have seen black magic and witchcraft and felt their effects. I have seen how the Light overcomes the Darkness. Through it all, the masters have never left me.

This book is the story of my journey. My hope is that my brothers and sisters may read the stories of my experiences and learn from them, as I have. They can know that those who have gone ahead of them have passed through times of testing, and they can see how they did it. The path will then seem not so strange to them. They can understand that there is a way to make it through all these tests.

I am especially writing this book for those entering the path of ministry—whether as formally commissioned ministers or simply as ministering servants to their brothers and sisters. They will face many challenges on that path.

I hope that what I have written may shed some light for the footsteps of all who follow and give them the assurance that with the help of God and the guidance of the masters, all difficulties can be overcome and the victory won.

I am grateful to have these thoughts and experiences available now in print. And I am grateful to Peter and Neroli Duffy for their dedicated friendship, encouragement and assistance in this endeavor.

May God bless each and every one of you on your homeward journey.

Chapter 1

A Serious Child

I was born in Ghana, in Patriensah, a little village thirty-six miles from Kumasi, the Ashanti capital where our king lives and where I am living now. My parents were peasant farmers, and I was born on June 25, 1932.

My oldest brother was Kwame Afram. He was my mother's first born. He became a fetish priest—a priest of our traditional religion, the Akan. The second was Kwame Frang. He became a taxi driver. The third was Kwadjo Beyie, a shoemaker.

The next child died very young. I don't know why my mother never told me his name. He was the fourth and I was the fifth. My family called me Kwame. Kwame is the name of a male child born on Saturday.

The sixth was Yaw Nsia. Yaw is the name for a male child born on Thursday. He was a carpenter. He took a long time in coming, so they thought that there were not going to be any more children after me. I had no sisters. We were six boys.

I was always very serious looking when I was a boy. I remember near our house there was a goldsmith, an elderly man. The goldsmith saw me one day laughing with some friends. He said, "Chee.* You can laugh?" When I was growing I was quiet. It was difficult to make friends with me.

My father was a priest of the Akan. There were many

---

* An expression of surprise in Twi, the language of the Ashanti.

different gods in our religion, and each priest had a name for his god. My father's god was called Afram.

My father loved me so much in those days. I was never allowed to be away from my daddy and I was with him all the time, everywhere he went. So I never went to school.

I remember very clearly an encounter with a man when I was eight or ten years old. I am always grateful to that man. To him I owe, I think, all that was to be my future. He was the headmaster of the Seventh Day Adventist school in our village. Apparently he had watched me following my daddy all the time. One evening I was following my daddy to town, and we met this headmaster.

He stopped us and he said, "Agya Kyei!" ("Father Kyei!"*)

Because my father was a priest of the traditional religion and the headmaster was a Seventh Day Adventist Christian, my father was startled. He stopped and looked at this man. The headmaster said, "Will you please give me your son, so I can take him to school?"

It was a very interesting encounter. My father looked at him for a while and said, "Okay, take him!" That was all.

The man said to me, "Tomorrow, come to school."

In those days, I had no shoes, no school uniform—no nothing. I had a piece of cloth tied around my neck. I went to the school the next day.

The man was keen. He welcomed me. He got me a piece of wood as a chalk board. He found a place for me in the classroom. There was just one room in the school for class 1, class 2, class 3 and class 4—about fifty students all in one room. All the teachers would teach in the same room and all the students would hear them all talking at once. I have no idea how they made it work. But it was good training because we

---

* "Kyei" is pronounced "Chay."

learned to concentrate. Later, the village built a larger school, with separate rooms for each class.

I walked to school each day. It wasn't far, maybe ten minutes, and I walked by myself. In those days there was nothing to be afraid of. In a humorous way, I would say that there were not so many bad people around.

Those who follow the traditional religion sometimes attribute the robberies, stealing and the things that we find plaguing modern society as being due to education and Christianity. In the traditional religion, people were afraid to steal—they thought that if they were stealing, their god would kill them. The Christians thought their God would forgive them, so they could get away with these things.

Of all my father's children, I was the second to go to school. The one who went before me did not try. He was not bright so he dropped out. That probably was why my father was not keen on me going to school. And because my parents were not Christian, education did not matter very much.

As I went to Seventh Day Adventist school, automatically I became a Christian. I was the first from my family to become a Christian.

Chapter 2

A Strong Woman

In our area polygamous marriage was a common practice. A man could have more than one wife, but he could only have one woman staying in his house at a time. The woman would stay the rest of the time in her family's house. My father had two wives, and my mother was the second wife.

My mother was a strong woman. When she determined to do something after very careful consideration, she never went back. She would not change her mind. I saw this in her confrontation with my father's sisters, who actually caused her to leave my father.

Everyone knew that my father really loved my mother, and because he was wealthy, his sisters were afraid that he would give his money and property to my mother, rather than to them and their children. That would deprive them of something that they thought of as their rightful inheritance in our matrilineal system.* So they were not on good terms with my mother.

It got to the point where my mother faced them and said, "Look, no girl or woman marries her brothers. But if you think you can turn back the clock and marry your brother, I am leaving him to you. Go, marry him. I will not marry your

---

* In the traditional matrilineal social structure of the Akan, the family line and inheritance pass through the mother to her children. A man's mother, his brothers and sisters, and his maternal nieces and nephews take precedence in inheritance to wife or children.

brother anymore."

They thought she was joking. My father thought that she wasn't serious. But my mother was very serious. She was forty-five. She wasn't going to bear any more children, and all of us were old enough to be okay if she left him.

After she made this decision, whenever my father would come to our house, my mother would drive him away. It got to the point that sometimes we, the children, were offended by our mother's actions. Why should she treat our father that way? But she was determined.

When my father saw that the situation was getting out of hand, he decided to seek help. He went to one of the sub-chiefs in the village, and the sub-chief called the councilors together to adjudicate the issue. I skipped school to go with my mother to this arbitration. I was old enough to witness all of this—about thirteen.

The sub-chief called on my mother and said, "You are here because your husband says this and this and this ..." My mother would not let him finish. She ran from her seat, threw herself on the floor and held the legs of the sub-chief. She said, "Please, stop this proceeding. I will not marry this man again."

In our culture, if you go down on your knees and hold a man's feet, it means you are begging with all your heart, with all your being. So the old man stopped. My uncles and aunts were there. He asked them, "What do you say?"

They said, "The person who is closest to the fire is the one who can tell how hot it is. She is the one nearest to the fire, and this is what she is saying. If we could persuade her to stop, it would not have reached this point. We have said anything and everything, and she will not stop. It is her determination." So the court of arbitration was dissolved. There was nothing they could do. My mother was left alone, and we went home.

My father still was not happy. So he decided to take it to

the government. It was 1945, and Ghana was then a British colony. My father went to the district commissioner, who was a British subject, a white man. He traveled from my village to the district capital, Juaso, where the district commissioner lived and had his court. My mother was summoned and they went to court. It wasn't a criminal case, it was arbitration.

The court interpreter read the complaint of my father. My mother repeated what she had done in the sub-chief's house. She ran to the commissioner and grabbed his feet. She said, "Please! No, I can't go back. I don't want to stay in this marriage any more." My mother didn't speak English, but she spoke in our language, Akan. The interpreter had to tell the district commissioner what she said.

White people are very particular about the issue of marriage, like any other tribe, any other race. But the district commissioner understood very well what it meant for a woman to do this. He shook his head, as if to say, "No way." He stopped. He did not proceed at all.

We came back to our village. My mother had won. But for my father, that was the last straw, the one that broke the camel's back. He decided to kill himself.

I don't remember the reason, but thank God, I did not go to school that day. I went to visit my father in his house. He had some very rich material, imported silk, that he would wear for important occasions, and he was wearing this material that day. There was whiskey on the table. He had drunk almost the whole bottle. And his eyes—I could see his eyes were all red.

It was afternoon, so there was no one in the house. Everyone had gone to work on the farm. My father picked up his gun, he stepped outside, and he started running towards the outskirts of the village, to a place where he reared pigs. He was singing and chanting war songs. He had the gun in a holster, and he had this beautiful silk band around his waist. Crazy.

I was just running after him and crying.

There was an elderly lady whose house was on the road toward the pigs. She was the widow of my father's uncle. I went to her house and I called her. I cried and I said, "Come and see the way my father is behaving." She came out, and she cried also when she saw him. She was calling his name. Then she ran after him. Finally she caught him, and my father turned like a dazed person and looked at her. Then there were some men who heard the cries of this woman, and the men came and held my father. One of them took the gun, and they said, "What's happening to you?"

When my mother heard that my father had tried to kill himself, she was surprised. I saw the color leave her face. She felt very sad. But this didn't do anything to change her resolve.

After this incident, a delegation from my father's family came to my mother. When they saw what was happening, everyone wanted her to go back to him. But she said again, "Let the sisters marry him."

As a child, I didn't know how deep the issue had been. I still don't know what my aunts had done to my mother. For her to act this way, there must have been something they had done that had hurt her very much. But with everything that happened, her resolve to have the marriage dissolved did not change. She married, she divorced, and she never married again.

GHANA

BURKINA FASO

Léo · Pó · Bitou
Diébougou · Hamale · Tumu · Navrongo · Bawku · Dapaong
Lawra · UPPER EAST · Zebila
Bolgatanga
UPPER WEST · Nakpanduri · Mango · BENIN
Gaoua · Wulugu · Gambaga
Wa · Wawjawga
Batié · Gushiago · Guérin Kouka
Varalé · Kara
NORTHERN · Djougou
Bouna · Daboya · Tamale · Yendi · Bafilo · Bassar
Sawla · Zabzugu
Gbenshe · Bole · Japei · Sokodé
Koutouba · Damango · Bimbila
Salaga
CÔTE D'IVOIRE · Blitta
TOGO
Bamboi · Yeji · Elavagnon
Bondoukou · Kintampo · Dumbai
Sampa · Wenchi · Kwadjokrom · Kete Krachi · Atakpamé
BRONG-AHAFO · VOLTA
Techiman · Atebubu · Kadjebi · Badou
Berekum · Jasikan · Apéyémé
Agnibilekrou · Sunyani · Ejura · Hohoe · Notsé
Bechem · Kpandu · Kpalimé
Mampong · ASHANTI · EASTERN
Abengourou · Goaso · Kumasi · Agogo · Ho
Konongo · Anyirawasi · Tsévié
Adriemba · Nkawkaw
Bibiani · Bekwai · Begoro · Dzodze
Wiawso · Awaso · Obuasi · Akosombo Dam · Aného
Enchi · Kade · Koforidua · Sogakofe · Lomé
WESTERN · Dunkwa · Oda · Keta
Asankrangwa · Nsawam · Shai · Ada · Anloga
Bawdia · Foso · Hills · GREATER ACCRA
Aboisso · Bogoso · Twifu Praso · Swedru · Tema
Prestea · Teshi
Tarkwa · CENTRAL · Accra
Winneba
Newtown · Elmina · Saltpond · Gulf of Guinea
Half Assini · Esiama · Cape Coast
Axim · Sekondi-Takoradi
Cape Three Points

GHANA

⊚	National capital
◉	Regional capital
○	Town, village
✈ ✈	Airport
—·—·—	International boundary
—·—·—	Regional boundary
———	Main road
———	Secondary road

0 25 50 75 100 km
0 25 50 75 mi

Chapter 3

To Train the Mind

After the divorce, my mother stayed in her family's house with me and her other children. My father was so hurt about the divorce that he would no longer pay for me to attend school. I remember my father said to her, "If you won't marry me, I won't pay the school fees of your child."

My mother said, "Never mind. If I need to sell my clothes to take care of my child's school fees, I will do it." That was a strong woman. She knew I loved school, and I was doing well.

I stayed in the Seventh Day Adventist school until I got to standard 4, which would now be junior high school. I was about 15. Then I had to leave my village and travel away to the Seventh Day Adventist boarding school. I had to go to Kumasi and then travel another twenty-two miles, so it was far from home.

I went to that boarding school for about two years. I had to leave in 1949 because one of my uncles had graduated from training college to be a teacher and he was posted to Juaben. He wasn't married, and one of my cousins and I had to go and stay with him and serve him. This is the way things were done in those days. So I changed from the Seventh Day Adventist school to the Methodist school at Juaben and later to the Methodist school at Nkawkaw, and that is where I completed high school.

This is when I took the name Paul. When I went to the Seventh Day Adventist school, the headmaster had given me the name Aaron, after the older brother of Moses. When I moved from the Seventh Day Adventists to the Methodists, I changed from Aaron to Paul. I preferred Paul because he was a preacher, very dynamic in his commitment and resolve. I preferred to be Paul the preacher rather than Aaron the compromiser.

After I finished high school in 1952, I should have gone to college, but because my mother did not have the resources I was not able to do so. So I went all the way to Koforidua to work for a relative of my mother. I called him grandpa. I helped him in his store, where he sold automobile spare parts.

When I was working there I had two proposals. A representative from the Methodist Church came and said they wanted some people to train as teachers. They had a teacher training college at Komenda and they offered me a scholarship.

Grandpa said, "When you come back from the college and you go into teaching, you will work as a teacher because you want money. You are working now and you are getting money. So why leave the money you have now and go to school? I won't let you go." In those days everything the elder said, you would do. So I didn't go.

Then the Seventh Day Adventists offered me a scholarship to train as a nurse. They had set up a new hospital. Grandpa said the same thing: "Why do you want to be a nurse?" He looked at the end product. "When you have finished all that training, you will go and work for money. If you are making money now, why do you want to leave?"

"But I want to train the mind!"

He said, "Hah! Forget it!" Again, I did not go.

But I wanted to get an education. For me, education was all-important. It opens the mind. I saw the behavior of those who had never gone to school and those who had gone to school and finished, and there was a vast difference between the way they thought about things. From observing life, I saw that you need to be educated to have a broad mind and approach to issues. I also loved being a scholar. So I had to take my college education the hard way, through correspondence. I was working in the day and studying at night, and sometimes in the evening I would go to evening classes.

Thank God the Methodist Church also helped me. In 1968 I received the All Africa Conference of Churches scholarship. This allowed me to attend a two-month course in advanced counseling at the Institute of Church and Society at Ibadan, Nigeria. It was quite close to Emmanuel College, where the Methodist Church in Nigeria also trained their Christian workers. When I went there I arranged with a tutor so that after the counseling training sessions in the afternoons, I would sleep over and take courses in Christian education and youth work.

I also took some courses with the Ghana Business Institute, and in 1974 I took a six-month residential course in business management at the Ghana Institute of Management and Public Administration, a UN-sponsored institute in Accra. There were a number of military officers also attending this course. At that time Ghana was under military rule.

Chapter 4

Grandfather

Grandpa had two employees, me and another boy. The other boy was unreliable, and grandpa did not want me to turn out like him. So he taught me to save money. This was one very important thing that I learned from him.

At the end of my first month there, he called me and said, "This is your pay." He took half and gave it to me. He said, "Take this to the post office, open a savings account. When you come back I will give you the other half."

Every month after that, he would put half of my pay on the table, pull my savings passbook out of the drawer and give it to me with the other half of my pay. "Go and deposit this, and when you bring me back the book, you can pick up the balance." He kept the passbook so that I would not go and withdraw the money. That was how he instilled in me the habit of saving.

I was with grandpa for one year, and then a friend of his asked my grandpa to loan me to him so I could take care of his photography shop at Nsawam. That was quite a tough thing for grandpa to do, because he felt I was the only reliable assistant he had in his shop. He offered him the other boy, but the man said, "No, this is the one I like."

Grandpa could have said no. But the bond of friendship between him and the man was so strong. So reluctantly, he sent me to Nsawam to work for his friend. To give me away was very difficult for grandpa. The fact that he did it showed me how close his friendship was with this man. Otherwise he would not have let me go.

In those days you could easily order anything you wanted from Britain from a catalog. You paid for it at the post office and it would come in the mail. My grandfather had once ordered a beautiful small stove. I was the one who took delivery of it when it arrived at the post office. When I brought it to him, I saw the way he looked at it, and I saw the joy in the old man's face when he got the stove.

When I left to work for his best friend, grandpa told me to bring him this stove. He said, "Kwame, you are going away. I like this stove so much, and I would not give it to anyone else. But take it. Whenever you are hungry in your new place, use it to prepare whatever you want to eat."

I was a bachelor, twenty-two years old. I was really touched by that little gift, because I knew how much it meant to him— and now he had given it to me. I knew he loved me and wished me very well.

It was at Nsawam that I met Elizabeth, my future wife. She was not from there. Her parents had moved from their town in the Kwahu Mountains, and she was living in Nsawam with them.

The first time I saw her was in 1954. I watched her carefully. I would call her and we would talk. At first, so shy. Her parents lived nearby and she was worried they would find out.

I watched Elizabeth for quite some time before I made myself known to her parents and told them that I was interested in their daughter. If they were looking for her and they did not find her, they could come to my house and ask. It was important for them to know that I had good intentions in making friends with their daughter.

21

In 1955, the Lebanese man who owned the shop my grandpa was running came to Koforidua looking for me. He asked my grandpa, "Where is that boy Kwame?"

My grandfather said, "He is at Nsawam taking care of my friend's shop."

The Lebanese said, "No, I want him."

So the Lebanese man drove twenty-two miles further from Accra to Nsawam to look for me and talk with me. He said he was opening a large shop in Kumasi and he wanted a trustworthy guy to take care of it. He had gone to see my grandpa and now he had come to talk to me. Would I go? Or would I like to stay at Nsawam?

So I said, "All right. You should return to Accra. I will consult my grandpa and I will convey the decision to you." But he was so eager, a few days after he went back he called my grandfather directly.

When I spoke with my grandfather, he said to me, "You can go."

I said, "Thank you."

This was an automobile spare parts motor store, a much larger one than grandpa's. It had better prospects than the photographic shop. So I went to Kumasi.

And I decided that I wanted to bring Elizabeth with me and that we should be married.

Chapter 5

Marriage

My father was a prominent person in our village because of his position as the fetish priest, and a lot of people came to him with their problems, including marital problems. In the years when I was always with him, I observed a lot and I learned a lot about marriage, even though I was a young boy.

So from the very beginning I knew that I did not want to go into marriage and then divorce. Once I married, it was going to be forever, as long as we lived. That led me to be very careful who I picked. The idea of rushing into marriage or taking on any girl who might come along was not for me.

In thinking about taking a woman as a wife, I said to myself that I would want a woman who would be respectful, not only to me as the husband but also to my relatives, my parents, my siblings. I wanted someone who was a Christian, who was industrious, not lazy.

When I decided to marry Elizabeth, I called my mother. (My father had died the previous year.) I said, "I am going to marry. This girl is living with her parents. She is happy. But I am going to ask for her hand in marriage and bring her to Kumasi, and she will come with me."

My mother was against it. The girl was not from my village. "Why would you leave this village to look for a wife? You have all these women here. No. You can't leave here, not even to go to another town within our area. Traveling outside our region, no." My wife came all the way from Obo. She is a Kwahu and I am Ashanti—we are from different tribes. But we are all Akans, so we both speak Twi.

My mother came to visit me in Nsawam. She told me that my uncle said he was going to find a girl for me from our village, so I should not marry this woman. She was serious.

When my mother and my father divorced, I was about 13. It was my mother who paid my school fees, did everything for me. I loved her so much and I respected her, but now she came with this message. What was I going to do?

We sat down. I said, "Mummy, you know I love you, I respect you. I don't have a dad who cared for me. You are my everything. But there is this question. The woman I marry is the one I am going to live with all my life, if that should be two years from now or three years or a hundred years. This is the woman who is going to live with me. She will prepare my meals. She will do everything for me.

"The one you say you want to find for me in my village, I do not know her. Even though we come from the same village, I don't know her. The one I want to marry, while I have been living here, I have seen her going and coming, I have met her parents. I know her well. So if I am going to spend all my life with a woman, why won't you allow me to make my choice?

"You women have very tender hearts. You listen, too. It is true that this is what my uncle said. But you are my mother and you are a woman. If you had not loved my father, would you have married him?"

She said, "That's a different issue!"

I said, "This is the girl I have found, and I love her and I want her to be my wife and the mother of my future children, if I should have them."

Finally I was able to convince my mother to agree.

Before she left, she spoke with Elizabeth: "Look, young girl, this my son, his uncle says he is going to find a girl for him in our village, but he says it is you he would marry. So I am leaving him in your hands. Take him to be your father, your brother, your uncle, your everything."

My mother got on the train and went away. That was the first hurdle in my marriage.

So Elizabeth and I were married. We performed the customary rites, and I formally married her before her parents and the Elders. The ceremony was in her father's house. My mother was there. I paid the dowry, which was money and some pieces of cloth. I would have been compelled to buy her a sewing machine, except that she had one already because she was a seamstress. The dowry, the money and all the things I paid amounted to about one hundred pounds. That was a lot of money in 1955. My salary at that time was five pounds a month. But because my grandfather had instilled in me the sense of saving, I had the money.

I was very excited about moving to this new job in Kumasi, but the girl's parents were a little bit scared. All over Ghana people were a little bit frightened of us Ashantis—warrior-like, too strict, we don't like nonsense. Her parents had said, "You are going to marry an Ashanti? Why marry an Ashanti?" And now I wanted to take her away to Kumasi. But anyway, that was their problem.

We were married at an early age, and according to our customs, in such a case a husband doesn't immediately take his wife to his own home. He leaves her for a time with her parents, and that is when her mother will teach her how to be a married woman. They have their own traditional way of instruction. So I left Elizabeth there with her mother in Nsawam while I went to Kumasi to find accommodation and get settled.

This was in March. Towards the end of the year, Elizabeth's

mother developed an illness and died. After the funeral, Elizabeth came to join me in Kumasi, and we lived happily there. All my children were born while we lived in Kumasi. For the first two, she went back home for the delivery. For the rest, she stayed in Kumasi.

My mother was good to Elizabeth. Whenever she delivered, I sent word to the village to tell my mother, "Your daughter has delivered." Two days later she would be in Kumasi. She would bring food and herbs to help Elizabeth heal after the childbirth. She was a good mother to Elizabeth.

A few years after our marriage, Elizabeth and I decided it was the time to take our marriage to the church and have a Christian ceremony. I told my mother this is what we intended to do. "Okay." We fixed the date with the minister.

However, my mother's cousin was a Seventh Day Adventist and she understood that this kind of marriage was different from a traditional marriage. She told my mother, "You say your son is going to have a marriage in the church. You know something? If he dies, the wife is going to take all his property and you will not get anything. So don't agree to it."

Less than a week before the ceremony, my mother sent me a message. "Come immediately to the village." I thought, "What is happening?"

I went to our village, Patriensah. My mother said, "Kwame, what you told me about your wife, that you were going to put a ring on her finger—I don't agree."

"But why? I told you this some months ago. You agreed. Now it is only one week before the wedding."

"I have been told that in a Christian marriage, when you die, everything you have will go to the woman. I did not know this. What about me, your mother? So I will not accede."

I said, "It is not so. Even if I die without making a will, according to the rules of the Christian church, whatever I have will be divided into three. One third will go to the wife, one third to the children, and one third to my extended family. That's you—my mother or my father. If both of you are dead, then I have no obligation to the other members of the family. If I like, I will leave something to them. If I don't, they will have no benefit at all of my estate."

She said, "No, no, no. I don't agree."

I went back home, sat down, and considered this very seriously. I thought, "She's after property." So I took out a life insurance policy and made her the beneficiary. I told her, "Mum, take this. When you hear that I am dead, take this to the company. They will give you this amount of money." My mother removed her opposition. I was married in the Methodist Church when I was twenty-five.

As time went by, my mother saw the respect my wife had for her, the services she rendered my mother whenever she visited her. Elizabeth was extremely good and humble and loving towards her. I remember a few years after we were married, my mother called me one day and said, "Kwame, if I had not allowed you to marry this woman, I would have done you a great wrong."

Some people talk about love at first sight. I think when you see a woman the first time and you say, "Oh, I love her, I want her to be my wife," it is not necessarily love. You may like her or see something about her that appeals to you. But I have found that love grows. It grows like a plant, like a flower.

It is when you start living together, when you serve each other, that the like you had is turned to love. Then you compare the affection you had at the beginning to the great love for each other that grows with time. You get to the point where if it was necessary for you to exchange your life for hers, you would do it.

So I don't believe in love at first sight and people marrying

Paul and Elizabeth on the day of their marriage
in the Methodist Church, August 1958

only for this reason. It's not good. Maybe for lack of proper expression of what one feels, we say love at first sight. But it is never really love at first sight. Love grows when it is properly tended.

In these troubled times, we see the modern communication systems that are everywhere—radio, television, the internet, many means we use to convey information to people. The natural inclination of the person who develops at a natural pace is tested strongly by these communication systems. People do not have enough time to sit down, observe and think before they make decisions that may affect their future.

If a young man wants my advice, I say to him, "Take your time. There is so much wisdom with our elders. Talk with them. Consult them and share their experience before you act, particularly as far as marriage is concerned. Because if you make an unwise choice and become involved in a karmic marriage, such a marriage will really test you."

Chapter 6

"His Service Your Delight"

My active involvement with the Methodist Church began in 1952, when I was in my last year in high school. Our headmaster was from another tribe, the Ewe tribe, and he did not understand the Akan language. So any time he had to preach a sermon, I would be his interpreter. He would deliver the sermon in English, and I would translate it into Twi.

That was the initial step, the beginning of the process that initiated me into preaching the word of God. I wasn't the one who prepared the sermon, I was simply translating what the headmaster had said, but that really planted in me the love for sharing the word of God with others. And I learned from that early stage that to be able to communicate the Word to other people, you must be part of the Word before you can communicate it. I had to listen intently to whatever the minister was saying to be able to translate it exactly. However, at this stage, it never entered my mind that one day I would be giving sermons.

When I went to Kumasi in 1955, I got fully involved with the Methodist Church. I was elected to head the youth fellowships. When the minister who was responsible for all the youth work in the church was transferred from Kumasi, they needed a replacement. That office was always held by a minister in the Methodist Church, but the superintendent minister felt that having run the youth fellowship very well, I could be the synod youth secretary.

That was how I came to be the overall head for the youth movements in the church in Kumasi, which included the choir, the singing band, the youth fellowship, the Methodist Guild, the Boys' Brigade and the Girls' Brigade. I was responsible for the annual conference and all the activities for all of these groups. It was a lot of work. At the same time I was running my own businesses and raising my own children.

After I had been doing this for many years, I felt I needed a break. I went to the synod and told them, "I have served as head of the youth movement for almost fifteen years. I don't have the strength or the time to do this anymore. I need to devote more time to my own business. I am raising eight children of my own. So I beg you, let me step down from my office and have someone else be appointed to take over."

The synod chairman asked me who I had trained to assume my responsibilities, who was ready to take the job. I did not have an answer. I had not thought of that. So they asked me to stay on for one more year to prepare someone to take over my position.

I remember we had a missionary from Britain, the chaplain for schools and colleges, Reverend Beresford. One time when he was on leave in Britain, he wrote to me, "There is something I think I have to ask you. I know that you run your own business, and then in the evenings you serve the church in all these organizations. How do you manage to run your business and to also serve the church in the youth movement and all of these activities? I do not want to discourage you, but I just don't understand how you do it."

I meditated on what I would say in reply. I took my pen and I wrote to him just a few sentences: "In the Methodist hymn book there is a hymn which says, 'Make you His service your delight / He'll make your wants His care.' That's all I know.

I care for the Father's work, and he gives me the strength and the wisdom to run my business."

When he returned from leave, this minister brought me a very beautiful book, which is still in my library in Kumasi. I found out from those years that if you make the work of the church your concern and help as much as you can, God and the masters will take care of your needs.

Chapter 7

Christian Charity

In 1969 we organized a youth conference at the Ghana Commercial Bank Training School in Accra, and I attended with other members of the youth organizations. I was thirty-seven years old. Youth from the church came from all over the country for one month. At the end of the conference, I was returning to Kumasi. Just fifteen miles from Accra, I had an accident—my first ever car accident.

How I had that accident I couldn't even understand. I wasn't speeding. Because it was drizzling rain, I had slowed down considerably. But all of a sudden, the car refused to be steady on the road. It started going in a zigzag manner, back and forth, until we hit a small embankment, which flipped the car over so that the wheels were in the air.

A friend of mine, a fellow youth worker, was in the passenger seat in front. A youth minister was in the back along with my wife's aunt and a little child. I managed to crawl out of the car. I opened the door and my friend got out. The woman in the back seat got out with her child, but we couldn't get the minister out. So I had to go back and use my hand to smash the rear window and pull him out through there.

Right before the accident a picture, a scene, flashed before me, something that had happened about a month earlier. Before I went to this youth conference, I went to my village. My mother had gone to the farm and nobody was in the house. I was getting ready to return to Kumasi when I saw my mother's three cousins in a line, literally running towards me and calling my name. They were asking for money: "Come, come give us money to go and buy food."

I did not know that they were the type of people who practiced night rituals. Innocent boy, I just gave them the money, and they went on their way. This was the exact scene that flashed before my eyes right before the car accident.

Still I did not draw the connection between these two events until after the accident, when my elder brother, who was the fetish priest, visited me. He said, "Look, Kwame, when you come to our village, don't give money to anybody."

"Ah," I said to myself, "now I see."

I said, "Thank you for the advice."

My brother wasn't there when I gave the money to these women, and I had never told him about it. But he was telling me in his own manner of speaking what had happened. Someone who was not African might not know about these things, but I understood what he was saying very, very well. These women used the money that had belonged to me to practice black magic against me. That was what had caused the accident.

And they did not stop there.

Some months later, my mother visited me, and she said that one of these three cousins had given her some cocoyam (taro) to bring to me.

I said, "Where is it?"

And she said, "I have given it to someone. But if you come to the village, go and say thank you to her, so that she will know that you received it."

I looked at my mother and said, "Thank you."

What she told me confirmed my suspicion about these

people. And it especially confirmed what I suspected about the one who sent the cocoyam.

Then I remembered that she had given me some cocoyam, many years earlier, when I was a boy of fifteen or sixteen, still in boarding school. We had a holiday and I went to the village. I arrived there late in the evening and when I went to greet this woman, she gave me some cocoyam. I ate it—God save me.

That night I never slept one minute. I was having a terrible problem with my stomach. I rolled on the bed in pain—rolled and rolled. I got up, sat down, got off the bed to lie on the floor. I was alone in the room. Until daybreak, I rolled and rolled and prayed for God to save me. In the morning, the pain disappeared. I think that this food contained something—only she could tell what it was.

When this happened to me as a young boy, I had a sense that she had done something with the food that she gave me and that I could have died. Thank God I prayed so much. I had come from the Christian boarding school and I knew the Bible, and I prayed hard that night. I think that is why God saved me.

Since that time I had always been suspicious of her. Then many years later, she made the same type of cocoyam for my mother to bring to me. If I had eaten it, I probably would have died.

Her son died in a similar circumstance. She had daughters, but this was her only son. He was a brilliant man, an accounts clerk at UTC, a Swiss organization that was one of the largest trading companies in Ghana. One Christmas all the young men went back to the village. We were so happy, and we had a jolly time there. At the end of the Christmas holidays we had to return to Kumasi, but my cousin complained that he was not feeling well, he had a problem in his stomach. We took him to Presbyterian Hospital at Agogo, and we left him there because we all had to go to work. It was only about fifteen miles from our village, so his mother and the rest of his family could go and visit him. After one week, we visited him in the hospital. His stomach was very swollen. Within another week, he was gone.

If I had eaten the cocoyam that this woman sent to me, I probably would have gone through the same process. If my mother had brought it, my wife would have used it in preparing meals for me and I would not have known it was from her. But my mother knew who she was and what she did, so she decided to give it away. This was not an accident—she deliberately gave it away. I don't know what sort of ritual these people perform, but since the food was purposely meant for me, anyone else who ate it would not suffer ill effects.

It is amazing to think that this woman could poison her own son. But she was a witch. They do not act according to logic or sympathy. It is their game. They do these dark deeds for one another. Someone did something for her last time, and now it is her turn. You cannot cross the line and take somebody else's son. But when it was required that she sacrifice her own son, she had to do it. That is their rule.

I had another experience of this kind of energy many years later in Kumasi. I had a neighbor, an elderly woman, who was quite troublesome. Many times she would come to me saying, "Brother, brother, brother, today I am very hungry. Give me some money to go and buy food." And innocently I would give her some money.

After a while I noticed that any time I gave her money, I had financial reverses. One day I sat down and said to myself, "I guess that I have to do away with sympathy and teach this woman a lesson." So the next time she came asking for money, I didn't give it to her right away. I knew about the teachings of the masters by this time, and I went inside to my altar and I prayed to God: "Father, you have asked us to show kindness to others, and out of that command I am giving this money to this woman. But if she should in any way use that money to do something that would cause harm to me, let that energy return to its source." Then I gave her the money.

God forgive me.

Three days later I saw this woman roaming around and talking like a mad person. She was dirty, she left herself unkempt. My heart jumped—I was so shocked. I understood the prayer had worked. She really meant something evil for me, and the energy had been returned to her.

I was on the way to town, so I stopped, turned my car around and drove back home. I went to my altar and prayed to God to forgive me for my prayer and to forgive her for whatever she wanted to do with that money that resulted in her problem.

After three days she regained her sanity. But I think that she learned her lesson, because after that she never came to ask me for anything again.

We need to use our Christ discrimination always in our interaction with other people. As I look back on this episode, I do not see that there was anything inordinate about the prayer that I prayed. I do not know how God sees it, but from my heart it was a genuine prayer. I wanted to do good, but I also wanted to be protected and not harmed as a result of exercising the gift of charity. And seeing the result, I also had to offer that second prayer from the point of compassion.

This experience proved to me that the teaching is true. It is lawful to ask for negative energy to be returned to the sender, and this is what the "Reverse the Tide" decree is for.* The Ascended Master El Morya has said that you cannot allow yourself to be a punching bag for people's negative energy, so it

---

* See page 289.

is perfectly legitimate for this to be returned to its source.

Since then I have made it a policy to offer a little prayer before anything goes out from me. I think I have a responsibility to myself, to my soul, not to give myself away. My prayer is a simple thing. "Lord, out of the flame of charity I am offering this. If it should be used in any way that will turn out to be harmful to my soul, please let that energy be returned to the source."

These incidents show the subtlety of those who practice black magic. The way that they approach you, it would never cross your mind that they might be doing this. You look at the individual and you think he is really hungry, he needs something. So you give out of sympathy, and that point is always very slippery.

Sometimes they are not even asking for something, they are giving a gift, as my aunt gave me food. That is another type of black magic. So it is always important to make the call, to offer it to God and also to listen to the inner Christ, your Holy Christ Self, for guidance. Black magic has no barriers from country to country, but it is ever-present in Africa in forms that you might not see elsewhere.

To be a Christian in Africa is not easy. My aunt, the one who in earlier years tried to do away with me, in her later years fell so sick that she was at the point of death. She was taken to the hospital. They saved her life, but then the question of paying for the hospital bill arose.

It seems that all the family knew what she was, and none of them was willing to help her. I happened to go to the town, and I was told what had happened. So I said, "Okay, this is my aunt. I can't let her stay in the hospital." So I provided the money to pay the hospital fees so she could be discharged.

One of my older cousins rushed to see me. "Are you a fool? Why are you using your money to pay for the hospital bill of this witch? You should allow the hospital to take her. We don't have any use for her in the family. When she comes home she will be very troublesome."

I looked at this man. He happened to be the family elder. I said, "But brother, can we really do as you say? How are you going to erase the shame in the whole community that your relative fell ill and you wouldn't pay the hospital fee? She isn't a child. She is one of the old ladies in our family. So I had to pay the money for her to be released from the hospital."

You see how family members can develop attitudes towards those who practice witchcraft, when they are known openly. To the traditional mind, this one is a witch, so why spend your hard-earned money to bring relief to her? If she should die, let her die. But then the Christian faith and the masters' teachings tell me what I should do to relieve others in difficult situations. I cannot ignore this.

I said to my brother, "You know the value of the Christian faith is to show charity. And the Lord Christ said to even do good to those who persecute you."

In Africa there are the traditional beliefs of witchcraft and there is also the concept that we also find in the law of Moses, "An eye for an eye, a tooth for a tooth." This kind of belief does not help the Christian to practice Christian charity. That is why I say it is not easy to be a Christian in Africa. Christian charity sometimes is completely at variance with what society may think.

Chapter 8

Finding the Masters

My first contact with the ascended masters and The Summit Lighthouse was through my preaching. I was appointed a "local preacher" in the Kumasi Methodist Church in 1955 after attending preaching courses and an examination and interview by the local leaders' meeting.

One Sunday in October 1972 I preached a sermon at the Methodist Church, and the whole place was full. When the service ended, a member of the congregation, Mr. Quagraine, met me at the vestry. He said, "Paul, the way you speak there is only one place that is good for you, that will help you, that I think will expand your knowledge and your ability."

I said, "What is that, please?"

He said, "The Summit Lighthouse."

"The Summit Lighthouse? What is that?"

He was a member of the Summit, but I did not know. He told me about Herbert Krakue, who was then the leader of The Summit Lighthouse in Ghana. He said, "Go to Accra, to the Volta River Authority office, and ask for him."

I said, "I will go." That was Sunday.

I had no knowledge about The Summit Lighthouse, no materials or books. But the moment he told me this, I felt so happy. I got home around one o'clock in the afternoon and got myself ready. I told my wife, "Tomorrow I will go to Accra."

She said, "What are you going to do?"

"I am going to find somebody."

That Monday I left Kumasi at four o'clock in the morning and I drove four hours in my car. By eight o'clock, I was at the Volta River Authority office. I waited there until they opened the office. I went in and said I wanted to see this man, Krakue, at the accounts office. The messenger took me there. I greeted Krakue and introduced myself.* "I have come from Kumasi to see you because I was introduced by Mr. Quagraine." Krakue asked for permission from his boss to take some time off work, and I went home with him.

We sat down, talked a little bit, and he gave me the first Summit Lighthouse book that was ever given to me, *The Overcoming of Fear through Decrees*. (This book later became *The Science of the Spoken Word*.) He said, "Go and read this." He told me about the Keepers of the Flame Fraternity and he gave me the application form. He said, "If you want to join us and study the teachings, you can fill out this form and bring it back to me later."

I said, "It is not a question of going and coming. Just let me sign it." I filled out the form, paid the fee, and I said goodbye.

By six o'clock in the evening I was back in Kumasi. I got home and immediately called my children (the boys).

"I am taking over your bedroom."

"Papa, where will we sleep?"

"In the hall. In the evening you will put your mats there. During the day you will roll up your mats and put them in the girls' bedroom."

I brought my boys into the bedroom and they helped me to clean, scrub the room, dust everything. I put a little table in there, covered it with a cloth and placed on it a picture of Christ

---

* In Ghana it is rare to use first names, even among friends. If you go to my village and ask for Paul, they will wonder who you are talking about. They call me "Kyei."

in the threefold flame that Krakue had given me. I put a candle on the table, and that was all. By eight o'clock, in two hours, I had a sanctuary ready in my house. Within a day after I heard of The Summit Lighthouse I had set up an altar in my home.

I started reading the publications that were available then. When I saw the quality of the teaching, I knew this was what my soul needed, and I wanted to share it. I started bringing in other people. Some of them were from the Methodist Church. We would go to church on Sunday mornings at the Methodist Church, and at four o'clock we would have a Summit study group meeting at my house.

At the beginning I do not know whether my wife really thought it would last or if it was just one of those passing things. But then she saw my commitment and the importance I gave to the teachings—it took precedence over all other things in my life. I think she was still undecided until 1976, when Elizabeth Clare Prophet and all the people came to our house in Kumasi.

Christ in the Threefold Flame
The threefold flame is the divine spark in the heart of every child of God, anchoring there the Power, Wisdom and Love of the Godhead.

Chapter 9

"Train Him Well"

When I joined The Summit Lighthouse, I was forty years old. I did not know the messengers Mark L. Prophet and Elizabeth Clare Prophet. After I joined, I learned that they existed and they delivered the teachings from the ascended masters. That is all I knew about them. Five months later, in February 1973, Mark Prophet took his leave of planet Earth. So I never did meet him. He was in Ghana in July 1972, but I found the activity in October. I missed him by three months, and I have only known him as the Ascended Master Lanello.

So Elizabeth Clare Prophet* is the one I came to know. She is the one who trained me. But before I even had the opportunity to visit the headquarters of the organization in America or to meet her in person, I had an interesting experience.

It was 1974. I was doing the rosary a lot at that time. Mother had released a series of New Age rosaries with prayers and readings from the scriptures. I had the tape recordings of the one-hour rosaries for morning and evening for each day of the week and I played them in the sanctuary in my house at six o'clock, morning and evening, every day. I showed my children how to play them even when I was away.

I remember one day I was playing the evening rosary—

---

* Those who know Mrs. Prophet as their teacher refer to her as Mother, in honor of her devotion to God as Mother.

I don't remember the particular day. I felt in my heart so much love for Mother. Even though I had not met her, I felt so much love. So I took my pen and I wrote a letter, introducing myself and telling her I so much loved the teachings and her, the messenger for the masters. I pledged my support to her and her ministry, and I said that even if it came to a point where I was required to give my life in order for her to be able to keep on living and teaching, I was willing to do that. I was willing to exchange my life for hers. I sent the letter to her by airmail.

After a few weeks or months I had a dream, a very clear dream. It is still with me, and I can still see the scene. Mother Mary came to me. She took my hand and she said, "Let's go!" I did not know where, but I was so happy that Mother Mary had asked me to go with her.

We went to a huge cathedral. The altar was at the other end, the communion rail in front of it. There was no one else in the cathedral except a priest who was at the altar preparing for the service. At the left side of the altar there were some chairs. Mother Mary took me there and we sat down. The priest turned around to look at Mother Mary, and Mary said, "Take him and train him." I turned to look at the face of the priest, and it was Mother. That was the end of the dream.

I knew then that the Divine Mother had entrusted me into Mother's hands. That was long before I ever met her in person. I realized then that she was the one for me. I did not know what this really meant at the time, but Mother knew at inner levels. She was my Guru.

Chapter 10

The Arms of Christ

When I first set up my private sanctuary, I set up an altar with a picture of the Christ standing in the threefold flame. After that, any time I had an appointment to go and preach in the Methodist Church, I would go to my sanctuary. That was always where I wrote my sermon. I would pull the chair in front of the altar table and place the Christ picture just in front of me so that I was looking at it. Then I would pray and write down my sermon.

One time when I was writing a sermon I found the Christ in the picture became very wide and drew me into his heart. His heart expanded and he drew me into that heart and enfolded me in his arms.

One of my daughters, Unity, is an artist. I immediately called her, folded my arms around me and said, "I am demonstrating what I have seen. Please draw it for me." I tried to describe as vividly as I could the image I had seen, and my daughter drew it for me: Christ with his heart and outstretched arms, and myself enfolded by him.

This image is always before me. And whenever I am in a difficult situation, somewhere I don't want to be, I see myself in that scene, in the heart of Christ, and I put on my tube of light. Then, no matter what the other person might do, it does not affect me. Any negative energy that might come through the other person is instantly turned back to its source. This is very real.

I still have the picture that my daughter drew. I have kept it close to me all these years. I have been afraid to give it to a professional artist to draw, because he might make a copy for himself and sell it. But now I feel it is the time to share it with the readers of this book. I trust that this book will reach the hands of those who really need it.

One Monday I was in my shop, the day after I had preached a sermon. I saw two young men from the Methodist Church and they were looking around on the street. I called them over because I hadn't seen them in that area before, and I said, "What are you looking for?"

They said, "Ah, it is you we are looking for!"

And I said, "Come in," and took them into the office.

I asked, "Why are you looking for me?"

"Well, brother, there is something that is worrying us and you are the only one who can answer our question, so please, don't get angry.

"We have been in this church with you over the years, and preachers have come and gone. But when you preach, when you man the pulpit, the message that we hear seems to be different from the rest. And what confuses us is that we have been here with you all these years, we have been growing together, but we don't understand how it is that your messages are different from the others."

I looked at them and I saw that they were sincere. They had come all the way from town, not knowing where I worked. They were just looking around the area and had found me.

I said, "Well, it is a private thing. But now that you have asked, I think it is my duty to tell you." And explained it to them in terms that they would understand.

"You know, I have a picture of the Lord Jesus in my house

Enfolded in the Arms of Christ

where I pray. And any time I have to prepare a sermon, I prepare with this picture and I pray. So I will tell you that my sermons are messages that are received from the Christ, because I have this picture in front of me and I pray." That's all I said.

They said, "Brother, thank you." And they left. And they were happy.

These young men were part of the singing band in the church. In the Methodist Church in Kumasi there was the choir and there was also the singing band. While the choir was made up of people who were literate, you could join the singing band if you had been to school or not. They did not normally sing from a hymn book. So these young men were not educated, but they were very happy to understand why my sermons were different from that of the "ordinary" Methodist preachers.

Of course, my sermons were also different because of the masters and their teachings. When I joined the organization in 1972, I bought all the books the organization had at that time and I read them. When I picked a Bible passage for a sermon, I would go to *Climb the Highest Mountain* and the other Summit books to see what Mother and the masters had said about the subject, and I would include that in my sermon.

Over the years I have really studied what Mother has said, her lectures, the teachings of the masters in their dictations, and the message that is contained in the books. It is different. You will not find it anywhere else. There are no loopholes, the gaps are all filled in. So these teachings are unique—they are very unique.

I call the masters' teachings the teaching of life. They come from our inner reality.

Chapter 11

The Church Must Survive

When I was a Methodist, there was a member of that church who was the head doctor in the Methodist hospital in Wenchi. His wife was also a doctor. She worked at the government hospital in Kumasi. The doctor and his wife had a problem between them, and it was not resolved before he died.

After he died, the woman wanted to make sure that some of his property reverted to her name, and she was refusing to allow his body to be buried unless this was done. She went so far in her determination as to swear the Great Oath of the Ashanti King, and the church members were afraid to do anything. If you swear this oath, no one will touch you. If people disregard this oath, it's big trouble.

There was a meeting of the leaders of the Methodist Church in Kumasi where this issue was discussed. They did not want to get involved. They were not going to bury the doctor. So I said to the superintendent minister and the council, "I want to contribute to this discussion. The doctor who is dead, who is he to the Methodist Church? He is our very renowned doctor in charge of the only hospital we have in Ghana. In our book of discipline, has he ever been disciplined in this church?"

They said, "No."

"Are there any complaints about him pending before the leaders' meeting?"

"No."

"Don't you see the error that you are making? This man was in charge of your hospital. There has not been any complaint against him before you, either in the past or even now. And now he is dead. Instead of burying him and giving him the full honors the church demands, you have allowed the widow to intimidate you by swearing the Great Oath of the Ashanti King. You are all paralyzed.

"I am an Ashanti myself and I give respect to my king. We don't discuss that. But I tell you, the church and God first. This is an issue for the church. This does not concern the Ashanti King. It is an internal church issue. So the oath shouldn't come in here.

"As far as the church is concerned, the dead man was a fully committed member of the church, in very good standing. We must do him the honor that he deserves. We are going to bury him as our member. If, after burying him, the Ashanti King has any problem against the church, let him summon the whole church to report. And we will go and meet with him."

I sat down, and for more than five minutes nobody said anything. The superintendent minister couldn't speak, the other ministers couldn't speak. They were all looking at me.

Then they said, "We will go and bury him. After the burial, if the Ashanti King thinks that we have infringed on his oath, let him speak not to you alone, the superintendent minister, but to the whole Methodist Church, Kumasi diocese. We will all go there to report to him."

So the decision was made and it was written in the minute book. The doctor's wife was not at our meeting, so they went and told her everything. After that, she was not very nice to me. The Ashanti King did not say anything.

The doctor was buried with full honors as a member of the Methodist Church. The following morning the doctor's mother came to my house. She knelt down and said, "Thank you so much. In the whole of the Methodist Church there was only one who had the courage to take this stand. Had it not been for you, the church would not have buried my son." His body had been in the morgue about three months.

I had told the members of the leaders' meeting when I spoke to them, "My concern is the church. We are human beings. We will die and go elsewhere. But the church must stay. That is all."

That was the dedication I felt for the Methodist Church, and I transferred that dedication to The Summit Lighthouse and Church Universal and Triumphant. This church must survive—not the individual.

My mind goes back to all the teachings the messengers have given us. What we are seeing in Church Universal and Triumphant is no different from the ancient mystery schools. As the light was opposed then, so do the dark ones come to oppose this mystery school and in very subtle ways to play their games.

We need those who have the courage and the love for the masters and their church. What I have learned about these shady ones is that when you push your chest forward and challenge them, they are cowards. You only need courage to back your commitment. That's all.

Chapter 12

The Master's Command

One day in June 1976, I went to the bush to visit a piece of land I owned there. I returned in the evening very late. When I arrived, my children said, "Papa, someone came here looking for you."

I asked them, "Who was it? Has he been here before?"

They said, "No."

"Describe him. What was he like?"

My children said, "An elderly man, slim, and he had piercing eyes. He entered the gate and asked whether you were in. We said, no, you had not returned. Then he said, 'Oh, then I am going.'"

And they said, "Nana, won't you sit down?" (In our culture, an elderly man is called nana—grandfather.)

He said, "No."

"Don't you want some water?"

"No."

"Okay. When papa comes, what should we tell him?"

"Tell him that I was here. I have something for him, but I will come again."

"Will you leave that thing with us?"

"He said, 'No.' And he went away."

So I questioned my children.

"You say you haven't met him before?"

"No."

"He has not been in this house before?"

"No."

"You know the old people in our village. Do you think he came from the village?"

"No."

Who could this be? I had no answer, so I just set the issue aside.

A few weeks later Mother visited Ghana. I came from Kumasi to Accra to see her. I had my experience with Mother and Mother Mary two years earlier, but I knew it was a dream. I had written the letter to Mother, but I had not received any reply. So I was not expecting anything from her.

I went to the airport to meet her. It was a Sunday, and there were a lot of Keepers of the Flame there. We were so happy that she was visiting Ghana. She gave the first thirty-six people she met rudraksha beads.* She had them all round her neck, and she removed each one and placed it around the neck of a student. I happened to be in the front and received a set of beads.

We took her to Odorkor, where Herbert Krakue lived, where we had the sanctuary in Accra. There were four or five of us there together with Mother. As we were standing there, she looked around and said, "Which of you is an Ashanti?"

I said, "Me, Mother."

She said, "I am coming to your place."

Krakue was a Fante, from the coast. I am an Ashanti, from the center of the country. Krakue said, "Oh, Mother, we have made arrangements to take you to the coast to visit the ancient castles."

Mother said, "No, I want to visit Kumasi."

---

* The seeds of the rudraksha tree are used in India to make beads for counting prayers and mantras. The seeds are often alternated with smaller beads of coral.

I was so happy. I was thrilled. I said, "I have to go back to Kumasi at once and prepare for Mother's coming." Mr. Afriyie drove me from the sanctuary to the airport. I took a plane and flew home.

My wife said, "You said you were going to a conference. Why are you back?"

I said. "It's all right. Elizabeth is coming to us. I have come to prepare to receive her."

That was Sunday evening. We did not have a real sanctuary. Our group was meeting in my house and I had cleaned out one room for our meetings. But I knew if Mother was coming we would need a bigger place. There would be a lot of people. So I moved all the furniture from the sitting room to the children's rooms and I had a big space available for the service.

At that time I was still in the Methodist Church, so I went to Wesley College and asked to borrow some chairs. Because of my very senior position in the church, I had no problem. So I set up all the chairs in my sitting room and prepared my home.

On Monday, I gathered all the Keepers of the Flame from Kumasi in our sanctuary and we were giving prayers and decrees to the masters for a long time while we waited for Mother to arrive. There were twenty or thirty of us in Kumasi then.

Mother, Krakue and a group of Keepers of the Flame from Accra drove to Kumasi. One of the cars broke down on the way, so they arrived in the evening, not having eaten all day. Mother and her party stopped to see us briefly that evening, and then I took them to the city hotel where they would be staying. We continued with our decrees in our sanctuary until very late, and everyone went home. On Tuesday we assembled again in the morning, giving more decrees while we waited for Mother to arrive.

By noon, there was no sign of her. I went to the hotel with

some of the other leaders of the Kumasi group. The hotel staff said Mother and her party had gone. We were puzzled. Where could Mother be? We didn't know where she had gone. So we went back to the sanctuary and kept on decreeing.

Around two o'clock, Mother finally arrived with all her party. Some Nigerians had also come and they were there with her. She explained that she had been with the wife of the top military commander in the area. The wife's brother was a Keeper of the Flame. The wife had taken Mother to see the Ashanti King, but she did not get to see him because he was not well. While we had been looking for Mother, she had been with the wife of the brigadier general.

Mother led us in giving the Fourteenth Rosary and then the decree to the Great Divine Director. After we had given it about forty times, we paused. Mother said, "Paul, come up and stand by me here." So I went and stood on her left. She called Herbert Krakue up, and he stood on her right. We kept on giving the decree to the Great Divine Director.

After a while, Mother said, "Paul, kneel." I knelt before Mother. And that is when I experienced something I had never experienced in all my years in the Methodist Church. Mother stretched forth her hand and placed it on the crown of my head. And she started making calls, invocations. One thing she said I have never forgotten: she asked Hilarion, who was embodied as Saint Paul, to lengthen the number of my

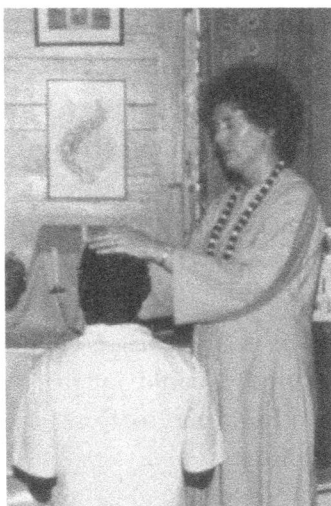

Elizabeth Clare Prophet commissioning Paul Kyei as a lay minister

55

years. And she called for his mantle to be upon me and anointed me as a lay minister.

There was a burning sensation from my head to my toes—like taking a very hot iron and driving it through a piece of rubber. I felt that sensation throughout my entire body. I thought that everything in me was burning up. I am glad that she eventually removed her hand. I felt if it had continued I would have turned to ashes. And tears—my shirt was all wet from tears.

That was how I got to know Mother as an individual with tremendous power to call forth change.

Afterwards Mother said goodbye to us. She went for a while and then she came back. She had forgotten to write the certificate appointing me as a lay minister. So she wrote the certificate, left it with me and returned to Accra. The next weekend we started the Africa conference at the University of Ghana, Legon. I was there. I came with all the Keepers of the Flame from Kumasi.

Later I learned from Mother about her experience when she arrived at my house. There is a wall around the house and a gate. As soon as she passed through the gate from the street and stepped in my yard, there was the Ascended Master El Morya, my sponsoring master. He told her, "Go and appoint that man a minister."

I figured out from my children's description and what Mother had said that it was Morya who had come to my house a few weeks earlier. He had something for me and he would return. He could not give it to my children. So he returned when Mother came to Kumasi and he gave me the mantle of lay minister.

Herbert Krakue was already an ordained minister at that time, and he had been consecrated by El Morya as a bishop on the Sunday that Mother arrived in Ghana. I had left for Kumasi and I did not know anything about this.

Krakue told me that when they returned to Accra, he asked Mother, "Did you know Paul before?"

Mother told him, "No, I did not know Paul, but the master knew him. And when the master tells you 'go do this,' as a messenger you don't ask him questions."

But it was a very sore point for Krakue that I was made a minister. He looked at my background in the Methodist Church. I was high up in the church leadership in the Kumasi district, I was deeply involved in church activities, and Krakue didn't have that experience. He felt I was a threat to his position. So he asked Mother to appoint some more lay ministers in Accra, which she did.

Chapter 13

Growing the Church

From that time on, our group in Kumasi was meeting in my sitting room. At times we had twenty to thirty people. Accra was the central point and so we got all the materials we needed from there—decree books, tapes and focuses for the altar.

I owned and ran two businesses at that time. One was an automobile spare parts business with four employees, the other an engineering services company with about fifteen employees. So I could afford to buy all the material. In fact the center itself did not use its money to buy anything. I just bought everything we needed in order to have the center in my home in Kumasi.

Our quarterly conferences were held in Accra, and I used to attend all of them. There would be between fifty and one hundred people there. We would play tapes of Mother's lectures and dictations and give our decrees.

Even though I was then a lay minister, I did not do baptisms: these were done by Rev. Krakue at Accra during conferences. I wasn't doing any outreach, but I kept praying and decreeing and the membership was increasing. They did not come in large numbers, but someone would walk in and inquire, and I would give them the Keepers of the Flame brochure and the form to fill out. The first thing they did was to join the Keepers of the Flame Fraternity.

I would plan my program for the church meetings on the

weekends. I bought all the tape albums published by head-quarters. I would play them for myself and select which lecture or dictation would be played on Sunday. I would listen to it ahead of time, map out the key points, try to think of the possible questions that might arise, and try to find the answers to these.

We would meet on Sunday afternoon for decrees and to hear the tape of a lecture or dictation. On Wednesday we held the Healing Service. On Friday we had the Ascension Service and on Saturday the Saint Germain Service. So I had four services in my home each week.

My wife, Elizabeth, is a wonderful woman and she didn't mind. I was still going to the Methodist Church with her. At the Methodist Church we would have Bible class meetings during the week. She regarded the Summit Lighthouse meetings as being like one of the Bible class meetings. I still went to the Sunday services with the Methodist Church, because I was the secretary of the Methodist Church in Kumasi.

Chapter 14

A Vulture under the Bed

There was a senior minister in the Methodist Church in Ghana who was once the head of the theological seminary there. After his term of service, he was posted to Kumasi as the head of the diocese.

The process for making an appointment is that the district synod holds a vote to elect who should be the head of the diocese. The result of this vote goes to the stationing committee, which posts ministers to various areas, and the stationing committee makes a recommendation to the national conference, which makes the appointment based on this recommendation.

In this case, the synod meeting in Kumasi voted for a particular minister to take this position. But the minister from the seminary wanted to have a position in the field after his term at the seminary ended. So it seems he spoke with the secretary of the Ghana national conference and arranged for him to tell a lie.

The minister from the seminary and the conference secretary were both from the coast and they were Fante. The minister chosen by the synod was an Ashanti, from my area. The Methodist Church in Ghana had begun at the coast, so the ministers in the church were predominantly coastal people. They used to say that we Ashantis have cocoa, so we are wealthy, we have money, whereas those from the coast are not wealthy. They regarded the ministry as their cocoa farm, and they did not want Ashantis to come into the ministry.

So the conference secretary went to the stationing committee, which posts ministers to various areas, and told the committee that the minister that the district synod voted for had said that he was ill, that he was not healthy enough to take that appointment.

The day before the national conference was the ministers' meeting. That evening I spoke with the minister who was chosen by the Kumasi district, and he told me what had happened at the meeting. The conference secretary told the ministers, "The Kumasi synod voted for one minister, but that reverend minister told me that he was not strong enough to take up the appointment. So the stationing committee replaced him with the one from the seminary." He said that when that statement was made, he was so shocked he couldn't speak. He had never told the conference secretary that he was sick.

I said, "What?!? At that level to tell that lie?"

I was so shocked. I couldn't bring myself to think of the fact that the conference secretary would stand before his fellow ministers at the ministers' council to tell them a lie. That was too much for me.

When this appointment came up the next day at the general conference for the whole of the Methodist Church in Ghana, the conference secretary said again, "The Kumasi synod voted for one minister, but that reverend minister told me that he was not strong enough to take up the appointment. So the stationing committee replaced him with the one from the seminary."

I think the president of the conference suspected that something was not right, that the Kumasi district might have something to say about the stationing committee overruling their choice. So he repeated the statement the conference secretary had made several times, and he was looking at me.

I was young, courageous, and with all the youth of the district behind me, I could speak out. He thought that I would respond, but I didn't. I was so shocked.

He repeated his statement. And then he said, "Is there any response from the Kumasi district?" I just looked at him, and I did not feel like saying anything. The shock was too much. So I didn't speak. And if I did not speak, no one else wanted to.

The outcome was that the general conference voted to send the minister from the seminary to Kumasi as the district chairman of the church. However, the process through which he came to that appointment was based on lies, so I had my suspicions about him from the beginning.

When he came to Kumasi, he was hostile towards me. One reason was that he knew that I was the leader of all the youth groups in the district and I had considerable leverage in my hands. He tried to replace me in the areas I was serving in the church, but he couldn't do it because these appointments were made based on merit. But his hostility continued, and we were not on very good terms. I actually did not give him my fullest cooperation, because he would have misused it.

He had a practice that was very unusual. Whenever he left the pulpit after delivering a sermon, he never turned his face away from the congregation. He always walked backward from the pulpit. In all the years I saw him he never turned around and walked away—he always backed away. I'm really not sure why, but to me that confirmed my suspicion that something was not right about him.

After he had been there for two years, I found out what it was. One of the junior ministers one day ran up to me in the vestry: "Brother Kyei, Brother Kyei, listen. This, your minister, is no minister."

And I said, "Shhh! What are you saying? What is your proof?"

He whispered, "He is no minister."

I said, "Why?"

"There is a vulture under his bed."

And then my mind went back to all the times I had gone to visit him at the mission house. He and his wife were living upstairs, and whenever I started to climb the stairs, the wife would say, "Stop! Stop! Don't come up! Wait there." I thought she was just being rude. But this young minister had gone up there that day and he had seen the vulture. He thought, "I must tell Brother Kyei," and he ran to tell me about it.

This senior minister kept the vulture under his bed—a live vulture which he fed. His wife was afraid that if someone were there the vulture might happen to come out from under the bed and come to the sitting room. That would be a terrible thing.

I know a few people from the coast, and they have a kind of voodoo or juju there where they use a vulture. Some use cats, others use different things. But he had chosen a vulture.* Even though he was a senior minister and the former head of the seminary, training other ministers, he was practicing juju.

Then I thought that I had been right to not want to receive anything from the hands of this man. Because of my uneasiness about this minister, from the very beginning I never wanted to receive communion from him. At that time I used to serve with the ministers administering the sacrament of Holy Communion. The minister would serve the wafers, I carried the wine. Whenever this minister was scheduled to serve the wafers, I went to the vestry.

I don't think anyone else noticed that I would not receive communion from him—if they did, they did not feel comfort-

---

* In the European traditions of witchcraft, such an animal is known as a *familiar*. The animal is the physical coordinate of the disembodied demon, spirit or elemental who carries out the wishes of the practitioner of black magic or witchcraft. In popular culture the witch's familiar is usually depicted as a black cat. The masters have spoken of the vulture as a symbol for the fallen angels.

able talking to me about it. Of course, the minister himself knew. But because he knew what he was, he could not ask me about it. Hearing this news about the vulture under his bed confirmed the feeling I had had within me—the dictate of my soul.

The hostility of this man towards me increased as the years went by. And eventually he decided to finish me with his black magic.

Chapter 15

For the Judgment

When Mother visited Ghana in 1976, a few of the members of the military regime that ran the country at that time were Keepers of the Flame. They arranged a meeting between Mother and General Acheampong, the head of the military.

The next year, Acheampong and the military proposed a new system to replace military rule in Ghana. This would be a combination of appointed military leaders and elected civilian leaders, but without political parties. They called it Union Government.

Acheampong said that people will not be elected to parliament on a party ticket. You cannot sit in Accra and say you want to be on the ticket of this political party and people back home will vote for you because of the party. If you want to go to parliament, go to your home area, where your people are. If they know you and they like you, if they want you to be their representative, let them vote for you to come.

Acheampong asked Krakue to invite Mother to come to Ghana again and he invited her to examine this proposal in the light of the masters' teachings. This was her third visit, January 1978. This time she came as a guest of the head of state. She stayed at the State House.

Mother supported the concept of Union Government. But the politicians and the university community thought this was a

Elizabeth Clare Prophet with General Acheampong
at Castle Osu, the residence of Ghana's head of state

strange idea. They wanted their politics and power blocs and they all teamed up to oppose it. And they spoke out against Mother because she was supporting it.

In those days there was no television in Ghana, there were no private radio stations. It was just Ghana Broadcasting. And because the government controlled it, these people could not use the radio against Mother. But the newspapers were really something. The politicians and academics were calling Mother all sorts of names because she supported the idea of Union Government. They said that she was meddling in the politics of the country.

That was the time that I came to have a taste of Mother's courage. With what the politicians were doing, one would have thought that any person would cower down, back off and disappear. But no, she would not. She had the courage to face the socialists and the communists who were so influential in our country.

Kwame Nkrumah, the first leader of independent Ghana, followed socialism. He took the country and aligned it with

Elizabeth Clare Prophet in Ghana, January 1978
with the Asantahene, the Ashanti King (above);
with the Ga Mantse, chief of the Ga tribe (below)

Russia and China. He set up a whole institute simply to train students in political ideology.

Mother appeared before the Socialist Forum. She told them, "Socialism is not a political system. Socialism is a religion of hatred. And it won't take you anywhere. It will not help the country." Mother was so brave—a very courageous woman. She confronted them all.

She even confronted the military leaders who had invited

her to Ghana. She pointed out the shortcomings of the head of state. He was fond of playing around with women. Mother stood before Acheampong and said, "Try to leave the women alone. Don't put yourself in a situation where you will compromise your integrity. You should meet with women only when other people are present, where the temptation to try to misbehave would not be there."

Acheampong was also a heavy drinker. I remember one day he was on a broadcast to the nation, and he was not aware that the microphone was turned on and he was live on air. He turned to one of the people there and said, "If I drink alcohol, I can speak rot." It went all over the nation. Mother told him that if he needed to drink anything it should be soft drinks. If he as the head of state would do that, the other military men would tend to follow him.

We had a messenger who was courageous. She would speak to any and all. She was really a mouthpiece of the Great White Brotherhood.* That was the visit when no master gave a dictation, except for Morya. The masters knew what a reaction this visit would bring.

It was during that visit that we had a confrontation with Horemheb. Horemheb was the commander of the palace guards in Egypt at the time when Mark and Mother were embodied as Ikhnaton and Nefertiti. El Morya revealed to Mother that Horemheb was the one who plotted a palace coup and murdered them in that embodiment, and that he was re-embodied as Akuffo, the second in command of the military in Ghana. Now she had to face him again.

---

* The ascended masters are part of a vast brotherhood of spiritual beings and angelic hosts that join hands with mankind to work for the betterment of life on earth. This spiritual order, the Great White Brotherhood, works with earnest seekers and public servants of every race, religion and walk of life to assist humanity in its evolution. The term "white" refers not to race but to the aura of white light that surrounds these immortals.

Acheampong was traveling from Accra to Tamale, in the north of Ghana, and Mother was invited to meet him in Kumasi. She was invited to the residency to have lunch with all the top military hierarchy. So we all went there: Krakue, myself, Mother, and the other members of her team.

After the lunch the military men stood at the entrance of the

Lt. Gen. Akuffo

banquet hall as we were leaving, and we were shaking hands. When Akuffo looked at Mother, he stared at her with wide-open eyes, very frightening. I had a feeling it wasn't right, but I could not say anything. That man had very piercing eyes and you would be very uneasy when he stared at you.

When we departed we brought Mother back to the hotel. I told Krakue, "The way that Akuffo looked at Mother, I did not like it. Why did he look at her like that?"

Krakue said, "Oh, that is the way he does these things. It's all right."

Mother explained later that this man was planning a palace coup against Acheampong, as he had against Nefertiti and Ikhnaton, and she had come to warn him against it. From that time, Akuffo felt threatened by Mother.

Akuffo happened to come from a place where there was a fetish shrine, not quite thirty miles from Accra, in the mountains. So he went to consult the priests there to get them to kill Mother, to summon all the ancestral gods and fires to finish her. When Mother felt this attack, she sent a message to her staff back at headquarters to decree for her twenty-four hours a day. She was battling with the demons and all the fallen angels in Africa.

What Akuffo did not know was that he was dealing with the messenger of the Great White Brotherhood. So he did not heed the warning that Mother had given. He carried out his palace coup six months after her visit. He removed General Acheampong and stripped him of all his military rank, all the privileges of head of state. Acheampong was not a general anymore, he became a private soldier, and he was exiled to his village. He came from the Ashanti area, a few miles from Kumasi. This Horemheb, Akuffo, installed himself in Accra as the head of the military, which ruled the whole country.

A year later, Jerry John Rawlings staged another military coup and removed Akuffo. That was a bloody affair. They took Akuffo and about eight military officers, tied them to stakes and shot all of them. They went to the village where Acheampong had been exiled, brought him to Accra and shot him also.

If Akuffo had not carried out his palace coup, I think that these killings would not have happened. But Mother said she was there for his judgment. It was thirty-three centuries earlier that he had been responsible for her death in Egypt.

A few months after these events, Sanat Kumara gave a dictation where he spoke of them:

> Now consider the example of your messengers and their mission to Ghana, West Africa. Three times I have sent them there.... On each occasion ... they effectively presented the incomparable Teachings of the Ascended Masters. Had these teachings been followed by greater numbers of the people, and especially the leaders, with honor and integrity, they would have averted, by the science of the Word and the love of the Holy Spirit, the great karma that has descended upon that nation.
>
> The messengers preached the Word to every creature from the least unto the greatest—the mighty

in their seats, the lowly in their huts. And even the betrayers of the people, fearing the wrath to come, sought the messengers' blessing (initiation). But they did not bring forth fruits meet for repentance. They did not forsake their old ways....

Thus it has come to pass that the Word itself is become their judge.... You see, had these men been men of God, their physical death would not have altered their souls' evolution; but from the moment of their rejection of the Mother and her admonishment toward moral integrity and self-sacrifice for the people, they stood self-judged before the Word....

Let none be dismayed. For when the Great White Brotherhood sends its emissaries to the nations, the judgment is come. Therefore let the Word that is sent forth lovingly be received lovingly and all will go well. Ghana is an ascended master nation. Until its people take the proffered gift and follow the Path that they have known of old, yet rebelled against time and time again, she will not fulfill her destiny as a community of the Holy Spirit or as the heart of Afra....

It is the deep desire of the Mother and has been since the earliest years of her embodiment to bring light to the Ghana that she loves.... The same table that she offered then, I offer today: Ghana, take the Teachings of the Ascended Masters and live. Do not depend on saviours, church or state, but let the Word itself—the true teachers, the ascended masters, and their true teaching—be thy salvation.*

---

* The complete text of this dictation by Sanat Kumara may be found in *The Opening of the Seventh Seal: Sanat Kumara on the Path of the Ruby Ray*, by Elizabeth Clare Prophet (Gardiner, Mont.: The Summit Lighthouse Library, 2001), pp. 186–90.

Chapter 16

Back from the Dead

The superintendent minister of the Methodist Church in Kumasi did not like it when someone else was popular. So one of the reasons for his increasing hostility to me was that I was very popular.

The bulletins for our Sunday services would be published a week ahead of time, and whenever it was announced that Brother Kyei would be preaching the next week, the church would be full. The downstairs floor would be full, the gallery full. The cathedral in Kumasi was very big; it could hold more than five hundred people.

Whenever I was preparing to give a sermon, I would enter my sanctuary, put the picture of Christ in the threefold flame in front of me and meditate upon it while I would read the Bible and pick a passage for the sermon. One day in June 1978 I was preparing to preach the following Sunday. I looked at this picture and the picture was talking to me. I wrote it all down, just as I received it. Everything I wrote came from the picture.

That Sunday I preached this sermon. An elderly woman was there. She was always at the hospital praying for the sick. After I finished the sermon, she came to talk to me. She was crying. I said, "Abrewa (old woman), what's the problem?"

She said, "Did you see? There were angels and colors in the room. Different colors all around. Didn't you see?"

I said, "All I knew was that I was preaching."

She said, "No, we were not alone. The church was all full of angels and colors."

I said, "Oh, I see."

The next day, Monday, this woman went to tell the superintendent minister what she had seen. This minister never liked to hear good things about other ministers. That was the problem.

The following month, when it came my turn to preach again, I went to the pulpit and preached. There was a Methodist Old Girls and Boys Association meeting following the service, so I cut the service short, we had the meeting, and we closed. I went home. Exactly one hour after I went home, I was outside in the yard and I collapsed. I think I came to talk to one of the children about something, and that was all I remember. I just collapsed. I was forty-six years old.

My soul left my body. I was happy, flying up—just flowing beautifully, floating. I was feeling like a beautiful bird going to this broad light ahead. I was enjoying the experience very much.

Then from the distance I heard my wife's voice, crying. I thought, "Who is this disturbing my wife?" So I turned to look at what was happening. That's when I returned to my body. I opened my eyes.

Almost everybody in the neighborhood seemed to be there. My wife was crying. The yard was full of people crying. So I asked my wife what had happened. She said, "You have been dead for thirty minutes." Looking at the crowd in the yard and even outside the gates, on the street, I can believe that it was so. It would have taken a long time for so many people to gather.

They helped me to get up and go into the house, to the sitting room, and I sat down. The people started leaving.

Then one woman came running. She lived in the area and she had come to see what was happening. Then she had driven to the superintendent minister's house to tell him that Brother Kyei had collapsed and was dead.

To her shock, the minister said, "Oh, I know, I know."

She said, "Reverend, you know?"

"Yes, I know."

This woman was so shocked. How could the minister sitting in the mission house say he knows that Brother Kyei is dead?

So she drove back, and when she arrived I was sitting there not dead. And she said, "Oh, brother, I don't know whether to call it a miracle or not. But you know, I have just come from the mission house. I went to tell the superintendent minister what had happened to you. He told me he already knew that you were dead."

Then I knew it was him. The woman who told me this also knew that this was his confession. I knew that he was playing at black magic. I knew about the things under his bed. But I did not imagine he would attempt to work his black magic on me. What reason could there be to do such a thing?

But there it was. He had tried to kill me. It was not just hatred: he consciously knew he was practicing black magic. And this person was a senior minister, the former principal teacher at the college where they trained ministers.

When he found out that I was alive, I guess he was surprised. I wasn't watching for his reaction. But after that I kept myself away from him as much as possible. Whenever he called on me, I would make excuses. He was the superintendent minister of our church, and I was a steward, so there was no way I could avoid meeting him. But I did not place myself in a position where he could have the opportunity to manipulate me, or to even shake hands with me.

A few months later, I was at the headquarters of the Summit, which was at Los Angeles at that time. I had a dream. Mother was sitting in the center of a circle of chelas and she was giving a teaching. I saw this minister chasing me with a kind of a horse whip. I ran and ran until I got in the circle where Mother was teaching and stood beside her. There was a big drum full of water. When the man reached me, he said, "Okay. I will get you another time," and he put what he was holding into the drum of water and left.

He was trying to get me again. He knew that I had found out who he was, and he wanted to kill me. The Guru had protected me.

Mother knew who these people were. Krakue once told me an interesting story about this. On one of the occasions when he visited headquarters, which was then at Santa Barbara, Mother asked about a particular gentleman, a lawyer, who had been a member of The Summit Lighthouse in Ghana. Krakue told Mother that the man had left.

Mother said, "No wonder—that guy has a vulture under his bed." Somehow, Mother knew. Krakue said he was really surprised that Mother knew about this type of voodoo they did on the coast, that there was such a thing as someone having a vulture under the bed.

Our Guru was very wise.

Chapter 17

Summit University

After the episode where I died and came back, I suddenly
lost weight and I looked like someone who had been sick for
a long time, but I gradually got better. About a month later
I received a message from Mother inviting me to come to
Camelot* to attend Summit University.

When I got to New York in July 1978, I visited a cousin
who lived there, and I called Camelot. Mother was not there.
I spoke with whoever was responsible and told them I was in
New York and that Mother had invited me to come to Summit
University. This person would not let me proceed to Camelot
until I had money to pay all the fees for Summit University.
I did not have the money.

I said, "My coming to Summit University was by Mother's
invitation." But they did not know me, and they would not let
me come to Camelot. It seemed to me that they must be strictly
following their instructions because Mother was not there. So
there was nothing I could do. I stayed in New York for almost
two months with my cousin.

Finally someone spoke with Tom Miller: "Tom, you have
been to Ghana with Mother. Someone from Ghana is now in
New York. He says his name is Paul and that Mother wants

---

* From 1978 to 1986 the headquarters of The Summit Lighthouse was at Camelot,
a 218-acre property in the Santa Monica Mountains, just west of Los Angeles.

Camelot

him here. But we have not allowed him to come because he hasn't got the money for the fees."

Tom Miller said, "Do you know he is Mother's friend? Those of you here, whose house has Mother visited? Mother has been to his house twice. It is Mother who made him a lay minister. Do you want to remain on staff? Let the man come immediately. If Mother gets to hear that that man has been stranded in New York for almost two months because you will not allow him to come, you will need to leave." I do not know who Tom spoke with, but this is what he told me when I got there.

It was in the dead of night when I received a phone call. I was sleeping. I picked up the phone and Timothy Connor was on the line. He said, "Is that you, Paul? Mother says, Come!"

"Where?"

"Camelot."

I said, "Thank you." I had my ticket, everything was ready. So the following day I jumped on the plane. It was September 1978.

When I arrived at Camelot, Florence Miller thought she recognized me from a picture from Mother's trip to Ghana. She would look at me and go back to Kali Productions,* look at the picture, and come back and look at me again. She wanted to be very sure that it was me. It took her three months to be certain.

I remember one day near the end of Summit University, I was walking towards the cafeteria and Florence was literally running to cross my path. She said, "Paul, I have something for you."

I said, "What is it?"

Then she pulled out the picture and showed it to me. It was taken in my sanctuary in Kumasi, when Mother visited there.

I asked her, "How did you get it?

"You forget that I work at Kali Productions. For the past three months I have been looking at this picture. I wanted to be very certain that I didn't make a mistake. Now I am sure you are the person in this picture."

Florence continued, "Did you know we were both made ministers in the same month and the same year?" Florence was born and grew up in South Africa, and we were both made ministers in September 1976.

"Oh, that's wonderful."

So she gave me the picture, and Florence became a very close friend.

At the end of Summit University the President's Reception was held at the Ashram of the World Mother in downtown Los Angeles. Florence was there and we were talking with each other. I was telling her that I was feeling very happy because after two months in New York and three months at Summit University I was going back to my family, my wife and my children. I missed Ghana. Suddenly Florence became stiff and

---

* Kali Productions was the branch of the organization that produced photographs.

she was looking over my shoulder. I thought, "What is she doing?"

Then someone covered my eyes. I said, "Who is that?"

The person removed her hands, and I turned and it was Mother. Then we all burst into laughter.

Florence said, "Mother, Paul says that he is very happy that he is going back home to Ghana."

Mother said to me, "Oh no, you are not going. You are staying with me."

My head started spinning, because I had never spent Christmas away from my family. And I couldn't accept it. I said, "But Mother, the SU rule is that as soon as the quarter is over, you must vacate the hostel. So I will have to leave."

Mother said, "Come and live with me at the Ashram."

Then I thought of a second excuse. "My visa will expire, and I cannot stay here without a visa."

Mother said, "Go tell those immigration people that your friends want you to stay a little longer."

I got into a little argument with Mother. But anything I said, she had the answer. In the end I had no more excuses, so I had to agree to stay.

Then Mother left. I said to Florence, "Why didn't you tell me Mother was tiptoeing up behind me?"

She said, "I couldn't tell you. It was not possible for me to tell you." And we all laughed about it. It was not her initiation to tell me.

When the immigration people approved my visa extension, one of the staff members said, "Paul, I think you have friends up there. Did you see the people coming to the class to take one of the students away? They took him away because his visa had expired and they would not give him an extension. But you went for a renewal and you got it." We laughed.

A few days later I was at Camelot and happened to meet

Mother outside the entrance to the Chapel of the Holy Grail. She asked me, "Paul, are you staying?"

I said, "Yes, Mother. I'm staying."

She said, "Good!" And she jumped up and down on the spot.

All at once, I felt like some weight had been taken off me. I felt so relieved. And I said to myself, "Ohhh, that was a test." It was a test, and I didn't even realize. It was a test of obedience —obedience to the Guru. And I was relieved because I had passed my test and overcome all the obstacles.

I thought of Jesus and his words to the disciple, "Lovest thou me more than these?" It was subtle, and I didn't realize what the test was about until I had passed through it. I had to place the Guru ahead of my attachment to home and family.

So after Summit University ended, I left Camelot and went to live at the Ashram, where Mother was living at the time. I was actually the first person to live at the Ashram. In fact, some of the staff from the Los Angeles Teaching Center* were a little jealous. They said to Mother, "We have been here all this time, and none of us has been invited to live at the Ashram. Now this man comes all the way from Ghana and you invited him to stay with you."

So they opened a little space in the Ashram for the LA Teaching Center to have an office there so they could come and go every day. These human character traits are there all the time, and you have to know how to handle them.

I was sort of on staff, working with the AV Department during the day. I duplicated tapes of lectures and dictations. I ran the duplicating machines, made copies and labeled them.

---

* The Los Angeles Teaching Center was in a separate building on the same property as the Ashram of the World Mother. Like teaching centers in other major cities of America at that time, it was a live-in center for chelas of the masters who worked in the city during the day and participated in services and outreach activities on evenings and weekends.

The Ashram of the World Mother, downtown Los Angeles

After I had been there almost a month, Mother let me go back to Ghana. I don't know why she wanted me there for that time. I think I asked Annice Booth, who was then in the Office of Ministry, and she said, "I don't know. It's only Mother who knows. She is the only one who can explain it." But I didn't think I could go and ask Mother—it wasn't what you did. So I just thought it must be some kind of training she wanted me to have.

I left Los Angeles to return to Ghana in January 1979, having sat at the feet of the Guru to drink of her knowledge.

Chapter 18

Leaving the Methodist Church

When Mother came to Ghana in 1976 and she and all the people came to my house, I was still attending the Methodist Church. Even after I was appointed a lay minister, we used to hold Summit Lighthouse meetings at four o'clock Sunday afternoon so we could all go to our own churches earlier in the day. The people did not find it strange to go to their own churches in the morning and The Summit Lighthouse in the afternoon.

After I went to Summit University and returned to Ghana in January 1979, I realized that I could no longer owe allegiance to any other group. So I sat down, picked up my paper and pen, and wrote a letter of resignation to the Methodist Church.

I said, "Thank you very much for all the assistance you have given to me. But I think I have reached a point where we must part." I was leading a Bible study group at that time, and the only church property that I had was the class book. So I said, "Here is the class book, and it is goodbye."

I did not tell my wife I had written this letter. I did not even discuss it with her. She did not know anything about it. I just wrote the letter and sealed it.

The leaders of the Methodist Church in Kumasi usually met at 5 p.m. on Thursdays. At half past four I drove to the cathedral. Only the chapel keeper was there, but he knew I was the secretary so he didn't think anything of me being there. The superintendent minister is always the chairman of the leaders' meeting, and as the secretary, during the meeting I would sit next to him. I went in, put my class book on the table where the chairman would sit, put the letter on it, and I went home. When my wife was ready to leave for the meeting, I said, "You go ahead, I will follow." She had no idea that I would not be there.

I understand that when it was time for them to have the meeting, they started without me. Apparently the superintendent minister read the letter, so he knew that I was not coming. He did not tell them. He said, "The secretary is not coming today," and he called on someone else to be the secretary. When they came in the agenda to correspondence, the minister said, "Well, there is a letter here," and he read my letter.

My wife told me that when they opened the letter and read it, for five minutes there was silence. No one spoke. Then they said, "We can't believe this. What is this all about?" They were looking at each other. Then the question went to my wife: "Mrs. Kyei, this is what your husband has written. Do you know anything about it?"

She said, "Please, I don't know. I didn't know that he even had this idea within him. He never, and I mean *never,* mentioned it to me."

"How could Brother Kyei do this without telling the wife, you, Mrs. Kyei? Where is he now?"

She said, "When I was ready to leave, he said, 'You go ahead, I will follow.'"

I had not told my wife because I wanted her to be completely clear. I wanted to take all the reaction on myself. They asked her and they could see she was completely unaware of what I had planned, so how could they get angry at her for what I had done without her knowledge?

My resignation caused quite a stir in the Kumasi diocese. In those days I was known throughout the country. There was no one who had served the church as much as I did. So when I left it was something.

After they had recovered from the initial shock, the leaders sent a delegation to my house, two men and one lady, to talk to me and find out why I had decided to quit, when, as they put it, I was "the pillar in the church" as far as the youth were concerned.

I remember very well what I told them: "Every person has the right to be where he thinks the truth is best represented."

"What does that mean?"

I said, "The Methodists have a term when a Methodist is seconded to another institution. They say he is 'permitted to serve.' Well, I am 'permitted to serve' The Summit Lighthouse from the Methodist Church."

They laughed and said, "Who permitted you?"

I said, "I permitted myself. I used my free will to come to the Methodist Church and I used the same free will to go to another church, The Summit Lighthouse, because I deem The Summit Lighthouse as a higher step."

"Does that mean that the Methodist Church is lower?"

I said, "I have not said that. Don't put words into my mouth. I said, 'I deem The Summit Lighthouse teachings as a higher level.' That is all I have said." So they left.

Then they sent a second delegation, and that one included the Second Minister. "Brother Kyei, why are you leaving us? You are the church secretary, you are a member of the highest council of the Methodist Church in Ghana, which is the national conference. You are known nationwide in Ghana. The Methodist Church is a worldwide family, and you are known even outside Ghana. The members of the delegation that comes from the British conference to our conference every year know you." They were trying to entice me with worldly things.

"Why do you want to leave all of this and join yourself to a small group? We understand that The Summit Lighthouse is such a small group, just about ten people."

I smiled, and I looked at him and said, "Yes, Sofo,* you are right. It is a very small group, but I am really happy being with this small group rather than being in the large family, the Methodist family. The large group has lost its attraction for me."

We sat and talked for one whole hour. They were trying to convince me that there was no point leaving that big church to lead a small group.

One of them was looking at me and I felt his energy, his vibration. So I told him, "Reverend, don't worry. I am as perfectly normal as you are. There is nothing wrong with me." He was startled. He thought I had read his mind. Apparently he was thinking that probably there was something wrong with me for wanting to leave the Methodist Church, with all its benefits, the connections, and having a prominent position in the community.

I said, "I know all that you are telling me, but my decision is final. I am going this way."

One member of the delegation said to the Second Minister, "Reverend, I think we had better leave. What ought to be said is what he has said. What we are, the largeness of the congregation, what we see on Sundays, all of this has no more attraction for him. So we had better leave." Thank God I made that statement, because then they left me in peace.

It was really a bombshell when I left. It rippled throughout the Methodist Church in Ghana. It went to the president. A lot of the church members had passed through my hands when I was working there. I was with the Methodist Church for about twenty-four years, and I was very active and fiery.

One thing that really hurt them was that I had passed through all of the process to be accepted at Trinity College to be trained as a minister and I had turned that down. There was

---

* *Sofo:* Akan word for a minister of religion

something that made me withdraw, but I could not tell this to the leaders' meeting. It was the fault of the reverend minister who was the superintendent at that time.

I had taken all the courses from Wesley College, I had completed all the exams and interviews, and all that was left was for this minister to sign the final papers. I went to him, and he looked at me and said, in a very sarcastic manner, "So you, too, want to be a minister?"

I sensed exactly what he was thinking. He was a Fante, and he did not like it that I was an Ashanti. So I went from his office to my workplace, and as soon as I got there, I called him. "Reverend sir, please destroy all my documents."

He said, "Why?"

I said, "I will say nothing else. Please destroy them. I have decided I am not going into the Methodist ministry."

"What? You are almost there."

"No. I am sorry. I am not going."

This was quite a serious issue and it shocked the man.

After about a year or so, he became seriously ill. He was admitted to the hospital, so I went to visit him, along with the most senior elder of the Methodist Church. On his sick bed, this minister asked the elder, "Please, I beg you, beg Brother Kyei to go to Trinity College."

I said, "Thank you very much, reverend, but my decision is final. I can't go." It shocked the man. It really shocked him.

I don't know why I was so determined at that time. But it was about six years later that Mother came and made me a lay minister of Church Universal and Triumphant. I told Mother I had almost entered the Methodist theological seminary but at the last minute I had refused to proceed.

Mother looked at me, smiled, and said, "Paul you were not meant to be a Methodist minister." Those were her exact words. And I believe that is true.

Some of those who were in my Bible class in the Methodist Church were already members of The Summit Lighthouse when I left the Methodists, but they didn't stay in the Summit. They eventually went back to the Methodist Church. There was no mass exodus of people following me.

I think that for those who are really steeled in orthodoxy, it is not easy to shift into an esoteric organization like the Summit. They can only come in and stay if it is their time and they are sponsored by their masters to do so. Otherwise they get enticed by the large congregation and the friends that they have there.

Often when I would meet people I had known in the Methodist Church, they would tell me, "We are praying for you. We are praying that you will come back."

I would say, "Oh, then you will have a long prayer to make, because as far as I am concerned there is no turning back. I am not coming back." They didn't know that the masters had just taken me. They were leading me on a definite path and there was no looking back. And I thank God that they did.

One day Elizabeth, my wife, was not happy with me being in The Summit Lighthouse, having left the Methodist Church. I told her, "Choose one of two things. I am in the Summit, and you still have a husband. If I had remained in the Methodist Church, you would have been a widow by now." So my being in The Summit Lighthouse is also for her sake. If I had been in the Methodist Church, my colleagues would have killed me by black magic.

There were two of the elders involved in this. There was a woman who was made the Sunday school superintendent. I was the Sunday school secretary and Sunday school teacher, and this woman did not like me. One day she made an insulting remark about me, a tribal slur about the Ashanti. I did not like it. So when we went to the leaders' meeting the following Thursday, I raised my hand. I said, "I have a complaint," and I told the meeting what that woman had said.

The superintendent minister addressed her very, very sternly. He said, "Look, in the world there are two types of people. There are those who, if you make them the head of any institution, they gather, they can bring people together and get things moving. Then there are those who scatter." And then he pointed to her. He said, "You are one of those who scatter." It was a fiery rebuke. This woman did not like me. She tried many ways to get rid of me, but she couldn't.

Then there was one man who was the secretary of the church in Kumasi. He was also a politician, and during one of the military coups in Ghana he ran away and went into exile in Côte d'Ivoire. That was when I took over as secretary. After some years he came back, and he thought that when he returned the superintendent minister should have asked him to take up the office of secretary again. But the minister didn't. This man picked a quarrel with me. He was older than me, but he was not civil in his words. He claimed that he should be secretary.

I said, "But why? You went into exile for six years. If I had not stepped in and become the secretary, do you think things would have been as you see them now? So what's the problem with you? If you have a quarrel about this, go and see the superintendent minister and go to the leaders' meeting."

In fact, he did go to make a complaint to the superintendent minister. The minister called me, and I told him what I said to the man. The problem was that I was in charge of all of the youth in the church, and they loved me because I was very active. I ran the singing band, the choir, the youth fellowship, the Methodist Guild, the Boys Brigade and the Girls Brigade. I ran two-, three- and four-day conferences where they would learn the scriptures, there would be guest speakers, and we really taught them how to run the organization. So the leaders of the church were afraid that if they said anything about

Brother Kyei the youth would revolt, and no one wanted to cause any problems there. So they could not do anything.

The worst was when that superintendent minister went away and another minister came to Kumasi in 1977. He was the one who tried to kill me with black magic.

All of this is why I told my wife that if I had remained in the Methodist Church I would have been dead and she would have been a widow. So she thanked God and thanked Elizabeth for having found me and made me a lay minister in 1976.

My wife believes in the masters' teachings very much. She is still a class leader in the Methodist Church. Every Sunday she holds Bible classes. She is also a lay preacher. When it is time for her to preach she will pick a text. Then she says to me, "Uncle, what do the masters say about this subject?"

We are the same age, but she calls me "Uncle" because that was my name in the Methodist Church when I was doing the youth work. They called me Uncle Paul.

So we sit down and discuss the topic she has chosen. I say, "What do you think about this topic from your Methodist background?" And she will tell me what she thinks, and also what the masters say about it.

The members of her Bible class in the Methodist Church used to say, "We thought we would miss Brother Kyei when he left us, but he has a substitute."

And even after I had left the Methodist Church, there were a couple of ladies who would come and ask for my views when they had a difficulty at the leaders' meeting.

"This is the issue there on the table. We know that if you were there, the issue would be resolved. So what do you say about it?"

I said "But I am not there."

"But it is not necessary for you to be there. Just tell us. We will go and do it."

Chapter 19

A Tug of War

After I severed my connection with the Methodist Church, I didn't go there any more on Sundays. I continued with the church meetings for The Summit Lighthouse in my own home. My eight children were living in the house, and now there were many people coming to services, and it was noisy. So we decided that we needed to move out and have a larger place for the group. Where would we go?

I owned a second house in Kumasi, which was rented to a Pentecostal minister, so I served notice for him to leave. I told him that I needed the place for my church. It became a tug of war. This man wouldn't leave. So I sat down to talk with him and try to make him see reason.

I said, "I have a church, and my church needs a place. Put yourself in my position. What would you do? You are a minister and you have your own church. You have space there for a mission house where you can live. I have given you a long time to finish it." He had had more than six months to finish his own house.

He said, "But your house has been a lucky place for me." When he stayed there his church had expanded, so he didn't want to leave.

I said, "That's good. But I also need a place for my church. There is nothing else that I can do." I kept putting pressure on him, asking him to leave. Eventually he left the place, reluctantly, but he was not happy about it. He ceased to be on speaking terms with me.

I now had to prepare the place as a church. I added a small extension to the house to make a hall that would seat about fifty people. I made one of the rooms the minister's office, where we kept our books and tapes and library. There was one extra room for the Keeper of the Flame who lived there as the caretaker.

The church in Kumasi still meets in that house. It is my own place—I built it—and I have allowed the church to meet there for all these years. In fact, in my will I have stated that as long as the church wants to be there, they will be allowed to stay and my family should not ask them to leave.

Chapter 20

Power Corrupts

When I first met Herbert Krakue, I did not have any special impression of him. I thought that he was someone on the spiritual path. I was happy to meet him. I was very happy to find the path. I was willing to help him. As long as he remained the director, I supported him. I even paid for his children's school fees. Each year he would drive to Kumasi, come to my shop, and tell me, "The school is open, the children need to go, and I have this fee." I would give him a check.

I had an inner feeling that I would one day take over his position. But I did not dream of that, it was not something I wanted. If this was a position I had wanted, I would have remained in the Methodist Church. What vexed them most when I left that church was that they were in a way grooming me for the office of co-president. In the Methodist Church, there are two co-presidents, one who is a minister and one who is a lay man. They were preparing me to be the lay co-president for all of Ghana. All of this I left.

So I was not interested in being leader of The Summit Lighthouse. But I had a lot of experience in church government, and I placed all of this at the disposal of Krakue. The documents, the publications, the constitution, the standing orders of the Methodist Church, how the Methodist Church is run— I gave all these papers to Krakue to help him organize our institutions. That frightened him. He thought, "If this man knows all of this, then he will try to take over my position."

I remember one day after Mother's visit in 1978, he told me that she had asked him to go to Liberia to set up the group there. Mother had visited Liberia on that trip, and President Tolbert, the leader of the country, had opened his doors to the teachings. He wanted Krakue to be there as the Bishop of Africa. Krakue wasn't happy. He didn't want to go. This is what he told me.

I said, "Don't worry. I will go. I will leave my business, let my wife and children take care of it, and I will go. Whatever period he wants me to be there, I will be there and help them." My offer was not accepted, and in the end no one went to Liberia. Krakue let it drop, and I do not know what excuse he gave Mother.

Rev. Donkoh was living with Krakue in the same house at that time. Later, after Krakue had been removed and I had come on as the director, Donkoh told me, "Did you know he did not like you?"

I said, "Why did he not like me? I have not done anything wrong to him. I was paying his children's school fees. Why did he dislike me?"

"When you offered to go to Liberia instead of him, he said, 'Ah! He wants to take my position.'"

"So that was all?"

"Yes. You take it lightly, but it was a life and death sort of thing to him."

I don't think of positions. Thank God that's the way the masters made me. I never struggle for positions.

The first time I realized that Krakue was not all he seemed to be was when he was going over to the church headquarters, which was then at Pasadena. He was going to be away for some time. I think he was going to Summit University, but he did not tell me what he would be doing. He had a car, and he said he would like to sell me the car before he left and leave the money with his wife and family. There was a loan for the car from the Volta River Authority, but he told me he had finished paying it off.

I said, "But you will need a car when you come back."

"I am not very sure when I am coming back."

I said, "Okay." He brought me the car and I paid him for it.

After he had gone about a month, Rev. Donkoh sent me a letter saying that Krakue owed so much money on the car, and if they did not get the money, the VRA wanted the car back. So I had to pay the VRA for the vehicle.

How could he lie to me like that? That was the first sign of a problem, for a minister to deceive me to that extent. But I still loved and supported him as the leader of the group.

In 1980, Krakue was dismissed from his role as Bishop of Africa and as a minister. Mother sent Annice Booth and another staff member to Accra to remove him. The reason for his dismissal was that he was playing around with a woman in the Ivory Coast.

This was a real surprise for me. I was living in Kumasi at the time, and I did not suspect him of doing such a thing. But when I heard this, I remembered that sometimes when he visited me in Kumasi, he would tell me, "We have a center in the Ivory Coast, and I am going to visit them and hold some seminars there." He was going there to visit his girlfriend.

Mother found out about this from Joanna, Krakue's wife. I think Joanna probably found out earlier and questioned her husband about it. When she found that it was ongoing, she wrote a letter to Mother. Krakue told me that he thought that it was Donkoh who encouraged his wife to write that letter and that Donkoh had even written the letter for her. I do not know if this is true. After he had been removed Krakue was bitter about it, and he tried to say things against his colleague, Donkoh.

Sometime later, Krakue and his wife became estranged, and Krakue left Accra and went to live in Takoradi. Joanna came to me then and told me that Krakue used to beat her. He would put her in a room, lock the door, push a cloth into her mouth so that the neighbors could not hear her cries, and give her a terrible beating. I think this was all part of his issues with women.

I was in Kumasi when Krakue was removed. I didn't see the staff members who came to Accra. It was all a surprise. They came and went back and I did not hear about it until later, when Rev. Donkoh told someone to come and tell me about it. Donkoh, Paul Lartey and Rev. Gbewonyo were appointed as an interim board to replace him. It was very challenging for them to take over from Krakue, who had been the leader of the group since its inception, for more than fifteen years.

One difficulty was where to meet. We had a beautiful church building in Accra at that time. It was built in 1976, for Mother's visit, and she dedicated it when she arrived in Accra. The problem was that it was built on land belonging to Krakue's wife. There were two flats on the land. Krakue and his wife lived in one, Donkoh lived in the other, and the church building was constructed in front of these. The interim board decided that they could not use that building any more, so they had to find another place to meet.

They first went to the Thomas Aquinas Secondary School at Cantonments, where they met in one of the lecture rooms. At the end of 1981, one of the members, the late Dr. Edzii, who was the registrar at the University of Ghana, offered the church an abandoned club house on the university campus to use as a chapel, and we met there until 1985.

When Krakue first left, he claimed that the church building

belonged to him, that he used his wife's money to build it and not the money of the church. Some years later, when I was the director of the church, after he and his wife were divorced, he came to me with many files and documents and the big ledger which contained all the expenses for the construction of the church building. He said, "These documents prove that I used the church's money to construct that building. So the building belongs to the church." He said we could take his ex-wife to court and claim ownership of the building.

I said to him, "Krakue, I thank you very much. But do you see what you are doing? Right from the beginning, when this issue could have been settled, you strongly denied that the building was built by the church. The church members said they provided the money. You said no. The architectural work and drawings were done by Rev. Gbewonyo. You said no."

Then I reminded him that there is a law in Ghana that whoever owns the land is the owner of the property on it. And since the church was built on that land that belonged to Krakue's wife, the woman had a valid claim on it. And now that he was not in the church, he wanted to saddle us with the legal expenses for challenging that claim.

"You are not here anymore, and the marriage between you and your wife has been dissolved. Now that you have lost access to the building, you want me to go into litigation, take the woman to court and claim this. We haven't got the money to do that. I will not do it. I am sorry. What you told us from the beginning is what I will go by. "

I had just taken over as director and I had a responsibility far greater than litigating on that building. So I wasn't interested. I thanked him. I put away the ledger. And he left. He was just wanting to punish his wife.

I never saw Herbert Krakue again. He tried to set up a rival organization. They met a few times. He even told them that

Mother had asked him to come back and take up his position as Bishop of Africa again. He claimed that it was because I didn't want him to come back that I had refused to write to him and pass on this message from Mother.

Krakue did write to Mother asking her to reinstate him. She asked him to account for the *Pearls of Wisdom* and all the other documents and files belonging to the church that he had taken with him when he left. "Produce them and I will consider your case." He had burned them all when he was removed. So Mother excommunicated him.

Someone came to tell me that Krakue had said that Mother wanted him to come back. I told the person that Mother had written saying that Krakue was excommunicated from the church. Mother said we should never allow him to enter the church, never let him have access to anything in the church. If he wanted to come back he should not be admitted until we received written instruction from her. I said that I had not been instructed to write him. What Krakue had said was not true.

When I spoke with Mother later about Krakue's dismissal, she said to me, "Power corrupts, and absolute power corrupts absolutely." So when he was removed, she didn't want to have just one man in charge.

All this happened in December 1980. Early in 1981, I received a letter from Mother saying that I should go over to Camelot. When I got to Accra from Kumasi on my way to Camelot, in my child-like mind I thought, "Let me go and find the triumvirate to tell them that I am going."

They happened to be having a meeting that evening, so I went there and asked to meet with them. They told me, "Sit outside. When we are ready for you we will call you."

I sat there for more than an hour. When they finished whatever they were doing, they called me in. I told them, "I have an invitation from Mother to proceed to Camelot, so

I am going. And I have come to say goodbye to you."

Rev. Donkoh was the chairperson of the triumvirate, and he said, "This is a personal issue between you and Mother, who has invited you. So it is not our responsibility."

I said, "Hold it. I have not come to you for money for airfare. No, I don't need anything. I have prepared myself. That's why I left Kumasi, I am going. But it would not be good if you here, as the triumvirate, don't get to know. So I have just come to let you know, to tell you that I am going. For Mother to have contacted us again here in Ghana, less than one year after our difficulties, you should have been happy. Rather than keeping me waiting an hour and then acting like this, you could have congratulated me. Anyway, it is all right. I am going."

Then Donkoh said, "Please, can we ask you to take this report to Mother?"

I looked at them and I laughed. "You think that this is a private issue between me and Mother. Now you want me to carry your report?"

Part of the problem was what Krakue had told Donkoh about me—that he didn't trust me, that I was ambitious, that I wanted his job. Donkoh didn't really know me, and he was not comfortable with me at that time.

But I did not mind. And his true character showed through in the end.

Chapter 21

A Dangerous Mission

I went to the church headquarters at Camelot in June 1981, and I spent several months there. In October, I attended Level II of Summit University, Fall Quarter 1981, Kuan Yin's quarter. The session started just a few weeks after the purchase of the Royal Teton Ranch* was announced, and Mother said, "You are going to stump all of Montana."

There were fourteen of us on the tour including the staff, and it was "Summit University on wheels." Our assignment was to travel all over the state giving lectures about the teachings.

We were on the road for eight weeks, traveling on two converted Greyhound buses. The Gold Bus was built by Mark Prophet for his family. The White Bus was the bus that staff traveled on for Mother's stump tours in the 1970s. I was on the White Bus, which had "Luxor" showing on the destination sign on the front.

The first couple of weeks was postering and handbilling to advertise the lectures. Then we went back to do the lectures, a

---

* The Royal Teton Ranch is located in southwest Montana, bordering Yellowstone National Park on the south and the Yellowstone River on the east. After the sale of Camelot in 1986, the headquarters of the church moved to the Royal Teton Ranch. Spiritually, the property is known as the Inner Retreat. Early in the twentieth century, the ascended master Djwal Kul prophesied that there would be established an outer and an inner mystery school of the Brotherhood. The outer school was to be on the outskirts of a large city, preferably near the sea. This was fulfilled at Camelot. The inner mystery school was to be in a mountainous region, far from the large cities of the world. This prophecy was fulfilled at the Inner Retreat.

The Gold Bus and the White Bus at Camelot
about to depart for a stump tour

different town every day. We got up at 5 a.m. and we did decrees on the bus. The bus was our sanctuary and our classroom, our bedroom and dining room.

The front section of the White Bus had three rows of the original coach seats, and we would hold our decree sessions and Summit University classes there, often while we were on the road. The center section was the kitchen. One of the students was designated to cook. She was the "Mother Flame," and she had the right to co-opt anyone to help her. She did all the cooking, three meals a day.

We slept on the bus in bunks. Behind the kitchen was the men's dorm—three bunks on each side. The women slept in the room at the very back of the bus and on bunks set up at night in the front.

Each evening was the lecture. We got there early to set up registration, book sales, AV and everything necessary for the event. People were appointed to do each task and everyone went about his business methodically. After the lecture we would pack everything back on the bus and have our evening meal.

One thing that really amazed me was that we never slept in the center of a city. We always drove to the outskirts, often to a campground where there were showers and other facilities.

It was quite an experience, eight of us living on this bus in a very small space, and a busy schedule every day from early morning to late evening. I had given quite a lot of lectures to conferences and youth groups in the Methodist Church, so outreach was not a new thing to me. But this was something else again. I enjoyed every moment of it.

One challenge we faced on this tour was that two vocal critics of the church were also in Montana at the time campaigning against the church, trying to stir up as much fear, hatred and anger as they could.

One of them was a former member of the organization who had even served on the messenger's staff, but he had left and was very angry with Mother—and a little paranoid. I heard that one time he drove his car to a Los Angeles police station and claimed that Mother and "these people" had planted a bomb in his car. So the police brought their bomb detectors and scanned the whole of the vehicle. They couldn't find anything except a few pieces of broken glass. One of the policemen told him he had probably run over a Coke bottle.

This man decided that he was going to try to destroy Mother and the church. One time he went to Red Bank, New Jersey, and visited Mother's parents. He claimed he was a friend and persuaded them to let him in their home to take pictures and do all kinds of things. I remember Mother in the Chapel of the Holy Grail when she told us all of this. She was absolutely outraged that someone would try to get to her parents in such a dishonest way. She stood at the altar and gave invocation upon invocation. The Guru knew what was needed to consume all the venom that this man was spewing against her and the organization.

The other person speaking out against the church in Montana was the mother of a staff member, and the campaign that the two of them mounted definitely had its effects. We had some interesting experiences dealing with it and the negative energy it stirred up.

In one city when we were postering, one woman came up and said to me, "Are you with these people?"

"Yes."

"Where are you from?"

"From Ghana, Africa."

"Aren't you afraid of them?"

"No. It is because of them I have travelled all the way from Africa." I later saw this woman hiding behind something, close to a wall, watching me. I thought, what is she afraid of? Does she think that these people coming from California are monsters, or what?

One of our stops was in Missoula, which is a university town. We postered at the university and all over the city a week in advance. But the day before the lecture, we received information that someone had gone around and pulled down almost all of the posters. So we put up as many posters as we could on the day of the lecture and we did our decrees to cut free the people who were meant to be there. We thought there would not be many people, but the hall was full and people were standing outside.

In Havre on the evening of the lecture, there was someone protesting outside the hall. He had a placard saying, "Don't go in. Go away," and he was trying to stop people from going in to the lecture hall. A journalist came and asked him why he was protesting. He said, "I am against these people."

The journalist asked, "What have they done?"

He said, "I don't want people to go in and listen. They mentioned Buddha, so they are Buddhists, and Buddhism is of the Devil."

So the journalist said, "What about the millions of people who are Buddhists in the East. Are they also evil?"

Then the guy said, "I am not talking of those in the East. I am talking of this group here. They are evil. And I have my children here in this city."

He wasn't going to go away, so we devised a strategy to outwit him. One of the students engaged him in a discussion, while others behind him directed the people to another entrance to the hall. When the lecture started we left him and we went in.

One lecture was in Livingston, the closest city to the Ranch. We did not have any serious problems there, which was something of a surprise for us, considering how virulent the campaign against us had been in that city. We thought that people would not come, but they came and the hall was full, even though it is quite a small town.

When we were in Helena for the lecture there, we went to the capitol building to visit a state senator who was a member of the Summit. This senator had been elected in 1980, before we purchased the Ranch, and Mother had advised him to keep a low profile. So we parked the bus away from the capitol and one of the staff members leading the tour and one of the students went to his office to visit.

Our team members discussed with him the situation of the campaign against the church. He said that there were some other senators who were also supportive of our mission, and that gave us a lot of encouragement. While those in Livingston and Gardiner had combined their forces to oppose us, we had friends in Helena. They were in contact with Mother, and they helped very much to cool down the hostility in the state.

Billings was the most difficult lecture of all. Before and during each lecture, part of the work in each city was to have a few people in the bus giving decrees to handle the opposition.

But in Billings, on the afternoon of the lecture, it seemed that this was not nearly enough. Every one of us, all fourteen, felt as if our hearts were being torn out.

One of the staff members called back to Camelot to speak with Mother. I don't know how they worked it out, but in a few hours they brought some postcard-sized pictures of Mother. They gave one to each of the students, and the picture had a string so we could wear it around our neck under our clothing. Mother's instruction was that we should all put these pictures on before we went in for the lecture. Mother wanted to be with us in a very tangible way, to bear herself the burden of opposition that was weighing so heavily on our hearts.

I still have this picture, and it is so precious to me. I have it on my altar. I wore it in later years when I was doing my television show in Ghana and dealing with opposition from the Christian Council, and I wear it whenever I am going out for an outreach lecture.

The hall was filled. I was manning the publications table at the entrance. One woman said, "You came with this group?"

"Yes."

"Do you believe what they are saying?"

I said, "Why do you ask me that question? Do you think that if I did not believe in this teaching and what they are saying that I would buy a plane ticket and fly all the way from Africa and then travel from California to Montana to join them? And that I would come here and sell these books to people?"

She could see that my temper was roused. She said, "I don't want to offend you, I am just asking."

I said, "That wasn't a sensible question. I am sorry."

She gave an excuse and walked away, and then she went in to listen to the lecture.

Lecturing all around Montana was an interesting assignment for a person from Africa. There were very few black people in Montana, and people could tell from my accent that I was not an American. My presence made them think.

On the few occasions where certain individuals approached me and made a remark that was designed to discourage me, I gave them a strong reply. They turned and said, "Sorry, we did not mean to offend." There was not anything that could offend me, but I always had a lion's heart and a determination to defend the guru, the masters and the teachings.

We had the strength to overcome the initial opposition to our mission. And when the people of Montana saw that we were not discouraged, they came to listen to our message. So it was really successful.

After the tour finished, we returned to Camelot. Mother summoned all of the student body and the community to the Chapel of the Holy Grail and she asked us to give our report. The other students asked me to be the spokesman for Level II of Kuan Yin's quarter. I said, "El Morya once told Kuan Yin, 'Kuan Yin, we must not fail Saint Germain.' So Mother, we want to assure you that wherever we find ourselves on this planet, we will not disappoint you. We will fulfill our dharma, our mission."

When I finished, Mother stood up and said, "You know, Morya has told me that he has never sent any of his students on a more dangerous mission than this Montana stump." Then I understood why our hearts had felt that way in Billings, what the attack was. Morya knew that it would be a dangerous mission, and I saw that without him, the energy would have killed us in Billings. It was a hostile mission—a very hostile mission.

In one city an American Indian had come to me and said "You are with Clare Prophet's people?"

I said, "Yes."

He said, "If you have the opportunity to speak with her, tell her that land is Indian sacred land. Do you think that they will sit idly by for her to come and take it? They will fight back. So if you have opportunity to talk to Clare Prophet, tell her this."

I said, "Thank you very much. If I get the opportunity I will do so."

When I arrived back at Camelot, this conversation totally disappeared from my head, and I never did tell Mother. Many years later she told the community that she had spent years making calls to clear the Royal Teton Ranch of discarnate American Indians. So perhaps she knew about this source of opposition without having to be told.

When I returned to the Inner Retreat in 1991, ten years later, I was really overjoyed to find that there could be peace reigning in the surrounding communities. We thought that they would gather themselves together, mount demonstrations and try to force us to leave. The way they were agitated in those early years, it was as if we were infested with leprosy. But the opposition was overcome, through much spiritual work and also reaching out to the local communities, an effort that began with that stump in 1981.

Since that time, I have done many outreach lectures in Africa. I would say that outreach in Africa is more difficult. There was real hostility in Montana from some of the people there, but we were many, so the burden was shared. With outreach in Africa, you are often the lone ranger, which is quite something. Montana was good preparation for my mission in Africa.

Chapter 22

Community

At the end of the lecture tour of Montana, before we returned to Camelot, we went to the Inner Retreat for a week of teaching from Mother. For most of the week, she taught from the book *Shambhala,* by Nicholas Roerich.

For one of these sessions, Mother took us to the Heart of the Inner Retreat.* While we were there she said she could see Maitreya sitting in meditation on one of the peaks above the Heart, and that was when she named it Maitreya Mountain.

Mother wanted us to sit on the grass, but the grass was wet. She had us turn and face the mountain, and she started giving her calls to Helios and Vesta, the great beings of light who ensoul our physical sun. Almost instantly we saw the sun come out—bright sunshine—and within seconds the grass was dry. We sat down and Mother taught.

After this teaching we were all talking, and I was telling the other

Maitreya Mountain

---

* The Heart of the Inner Retreat is a beautiful valley, high in the mountains, that is the spiritual center of the Royal Teton Ranch.

The Heart of the Inner Retreat

students the story of how I had received a picture of Saladin, the Muslim ruler and general at the time of the Crusades.

There was a Keeper of the Flame in our group in Ghana who was a major in the military. He had been sent for peacekeeping duties in the Middle East, on the border of Lebanon and Israel. He took some time off and visited Israel and went to a museum, where he saw exhibits about Saladin. He brought me a very beautiful portrait of him. I asked him who Saladin was, because I had not heard of him. I told the other students that I was really wondering why he had brought me these things having to do with Saladin. And then in that quarter we heard Mother's teachings about Saladin and I learned that this had been an embodiment of Mark Prophet, now the Ascended Master Lanello.

Mother was sitting quite some distance away, and we didn't know that she was listening to what we were saying. But then she said, "Paul, now you know who invited you here." So it was Lanello who invited me to Summit University. I had no idea of this connection until she said this. I only knew that Mother had invited me.

Then Mother added, "Paul, that is why I want you to go back to Ghana and organize the Accra group, as the director." That was in front of everyone in the Heart of the Inner Retreat. And I thought, "What a headache that will be!"

Krakue had been excommunicated and some of the students left the church and followed him when he tried to set up a rival group. So there was division. I said to myself, "With this kind of tattered group, how am I going to weld them together in Accra?" But thank God for the opportunity that the Methodist Church gave me with the youth work and running the youth organization. I knew how to bring people together, and I have the patience to listen to all the "nonsense" that others do not want to listen to. So I had that preparation from that level.

During that Summit University quarter, we also heard Mother's teachings on *Community,* another book by the Roerichs. These teachings moved me very much, because I was thinking of rebuilding. Since Mother told me to put the Accra group together again, my attention was very much on trying to build community.

Those teachings by Mother are now a book, *Community: A Journey to the Heart of Spiritual Community.* I have studied it, and I used to teach from it in the group in Accra. On one visit to South Africa we spent a whole week studying it. South Africa also has the problem of interracial tensions, and community is a very good subject for them to understand.

Morya had a purpose in bringing forth the teachings on community—both the writings of the Roerichs and Mother's commentary. He was drawing attention to what had been before. When Mother teaches on these kinds of subjects, I try to go to the inner recesses of the mind, to see what I can remember. These teachings on community rekindled in me a memory of the joy of living together in true community.

When you approach the teaching in this way, the message

sinks in deeply, and you don't forget. That is one reason I enjoy the ascended masters' teachings so much. I still love those teachings on community. As for Shamballa, I think of it with a great awe.* I find my mind struggling to find out what happened, what are the lessons we have to revisit in that episode.

My ordination as a minister happened while I was at the Inner Retreat. It was an inner experience, and I did not even realize the implication of it at the time. All I knew was that there was a big garden at inner levels and Morya officiated at a ceremony. I woke from that dream singing a song to El Morya, "Master Morya, Beloved."

I did not know what it meant. However, after I returned to Ghana I wrote to Mother asking for further training. She wrote back to me: "I have no other training for you. You have been trained by Morya. You have been ordained by Morya. Use your title. The people should call you Reverend Kyei."

There was no outer ceremony of ordination. There was no certificate, just the letter from Mother. But I remember the ceremony from inner levels very clearly. I did not understand the ceremony when I was experiencing it. But when Mother sent

---

* In Tibetan Buddhist tradition, Shamballa is a kingdom in Central Asia, the seat of a great king who will come forth in an age of darkness to vanquish the forces of evil and usher in a golden age. The ascended masters teach that this ancient focus of light was once a physical city on the White Island in the Gobi Sea (now the Gobi Desert). No longer physical, it is the etheric retreat of Sanat Kumara and Gautama Buddha, the Lord of the World. Nicholas Roerich wrote extensively of Shamballa and its significance in the spiritual transformation of the planet.

In 1991 Elizabeth Clare Prophet spoke of the time when the physical city and retreat at Shamballa were withdrawn to the etheric plane. "The city of Shamballa was intact in the physical octave in the island in the Gobi Sea about 9400 B.C. We visit at the moment that the scene is shown to us.... Sanat Kumara is leading a holy chant in an unknown tongue. Suddenly the atmosphere is broken by raucous cries and derisive laughter. They belong to a group who call themselves the 'Realists.' They no longer remember their home on Venus. They prefer to call it a religious myth. They make up 50 percent of Shamballa's population....

"Suddenly ... the city, the temple and all of the participants in this ceremony disappear from view. The Realists, including the group which had disturbed the ceremony, find themselves standing in the middle of a desert. The beautiful gardens and vegetation that surrounded the city have also disappeared. They live out the rest of their days as nomads." [*Pearls of Wisdom*, vol. 47, no. 5, February 1, 2004]

me the letter I understood.

I had a similar experience once more when I visited the Inner Retreat in 2001. It was the night before I had a meeting with the presidents of the church. I was trying to sleep, but I think at that time I was not deeply asleep. I saw the same kind of ceremony. The Ascended Master Afra was there, the master who sponsors the continent and the people of Africa. He said to Morya, "Friend, please perform the ceremony for me." And Lanello said, "Morya, I will join you." It was a ceremony by Afra, Morya and Lanello, a great ceremony, and there was a big gathering. I knelt down. What they were saying, I did not hear, but there were many invocations, a lot of calls. When they finished, Lanello said, "The ancient mantle is restored."

I asked him, "What mantle?" Then I saw immediately a scene that was shown me in 1982 when I was administering Holy Communion to a girl in our Sunday school in Accra. I had picked up the wafer, dropped it on the tongue of this little girl, and a kind of a veil parted. I saw myself in ministerial robes with a Maltese cross on the front and back and a violet girdle. I was administering the same Holy Communion to the same soul in the Temple at Luxor in Egypt. We were in an outer temple, facing the Nile.

The day after the dream, when I was meeting with the presidents, I told them about this service at Luxor and the ceremony I went through the night before. And then I said, "I have been wondering what I did not do right long ago that they sent me back to this embodiment." They looked at me, and they smiled and said, "This time, Paul, we will help you to make it."

Then we spoke about my being a regional minister. I had discussed this earlier with the head of the Office of Ministry, and she had asked me to be the regional minister for Africa. She came in and signed my appointment letter. I thought about what it means to be a regional minister. To be responsible for a region and the other ministers in a region is the office of a bishop. I said, "Is this equivalent of a bishop?" And the presidents said, "Yes." Even though the office of bishop no longer appears in our articles and bylaws, that is what it would be called in another church. And I smiled because then I understood the meaning of the ceremony the previous night.

It was an inner thing. I wanted to keep it to myself—because I didn't know all the implications. I also learned from the Guru that there are certain experiences that are between the master and the chela and should remain private. However, now that I have the opportunity to leave behind a record of my life, I believe it is time to share this experience. We all have our experiences, inner and outer, with our God. This is not limited to me alone. I share this episode from my path in the hope that in reading of it, others may be encouraged in their own walk with the masters.

When I returned to Ghana I had someone make for me the robe with the Maltese cross that I had seen. When I put on that Maltese cross, I felt the weight within me. I felt I had become too serious for my liking. In fact, I became frightened. So I took it off and I did not put it on again for many years. To those who are inquisitive enough, who dare ask me, I say, bishop is not a term that is used now in our church. The office of bishop is not outer in this embodiment, not something that anyone gave to me. It is something that I brought with me.

One day I was in Kenya in the airport going through the line, and the security man who was there looked at me and the long line of people and said, "Please, Bishop, come." I walked past the others and he said, "You are a bishop?" I said "Yes." I was not wearing a robe, but somehow he knew.

Chapter 23

The Gods of My Father

As much as my father loved me when I was a young child, whenever he would invite me to the shrine of his gods, I would not go. My mother would go to the shrine, and she would bring back pieces of kola, ostensibly having been blessed by the priest. You would chew the kola nut and it was supposed to give you spiritual protection. When my mother would bring it, I would throw it back at her, even when I was very young. I did not want to have anything to do with it—ever. I was very aware of that.

The last time I threw the kola at her, I was about thirteen. My mother was so eager to give it to me she didn't even wait until she got into the house. We were on the street, and when I threw the kola back at her, she cried out, "My son, you will die early if you do this."

All my family used to go to the shrine. They would take the kola from the shrine. Sometimes the priest would use clay to mark their foreheads. They believed that these things gave them protection from witchcraft and evil spirits. So if you were in such a family and refused to be part of this sort of ritual, they thought you wouldn't have long to live. But if she were living today, my mother would see that of all her six children, I am the only one surviving.

In our African culture, people believe in witchcraft. It's like their religion. Even those who don't practice it believe it exists and that they need to protect themselves from it. They believe it causes so much harm—and this is true. Witchcraft does exist, and it can cause real harm. If you believe in those kinds of practices and you get overcome by the fear of them, they really have control over you.

Witchcraft really permeates the culture in Africa. If you turn on the TV in Ghana, there are certain television stations that give access to what we call "one-man churches." Most of the stations don't give air time to those who go into excess, but there are a few television stations, and more are springing up, who allow such people access because they want the money— these churches pay for the air time. And all they preach is deliverance from witchcraft.

On these programs you see hundreds of people congregating, and the ministers say they are working "miracles." Sometimes it is so revolting, you can't even watch. They pollute the mind. Once in a while someone comes out to expose these pastors, how they pay people money to say that they were healed. This is something that goes on almost all the time.

So the belief goes both ways. The people believe in witchcraft and they also believe in those who claim that they can exorcise this from the individuals who are possessed. And I think these beliefs have grown to the extent that they have even paralyzed the people.

Africa is not the only place where there is witchcraft. In Britain they have witches' festivals where they perform the ceremonies of witchcraft. There is the Church of Satan in America. There is voodoo in the Caribbean and Central America. It's all part of the fallen ones' trap to have their own pseudo-religion to confuse and manipulate people. For those who take witchcraft as their religion and believe in it, by that belief they give more power to it. The child of the light would not believe in it. But to merely not believe in it is sometimes not enough. It is also necessary to invoke the Science of the Spoken Word to challenge its manifestation. Then one can walk through it unscathed.

What I did learn from the traditionalists is truthfulness. But they tell the truth not because they want to, but out of fear. They are afraid that if they tell a lie, their god will kill them. So out of fear, they try to be truthful.

When I think of where I came from, and then I see the image of Luxor always before me, the ascension temple, this really sets me thinking. If I was a priest in that temple long ago, and coming back into this life, they planted me in the home of these traditional worshippers, what was my error or betrayal or whatever it was? What had I done that they should plant me there to see whether I could come out of that pit?

I call it a pit, and it is true. How could you come from the altar of the Most High, the altar of Light, to a religion where they sacrifice animals—from one extreme to the other? And how do you get out of this? And yet I did.

I had an uncle I was staying with when he completed training college. Before he passed on two or three years ago, anytime he met me, he would stand back and say, "Kyei, there are real wonders in the world. How can a son of a fetish priest become a minister of the gospel?" He used to see my television programs and listen to my radio broadcasts. "I can't believe it. God is indeed wonderful," that was his refrain. Whenever he saw me, he would tell his friends, "God is wonderful. This, my nephew, the son of a fetish priest, becoming a minister of the gospel!"

Sometimes what I say is, "God and the masters know the reason I was born where I was." And I think my soul is so grateful that they let me experience both extremes—serving the Light and also being born into a home where, even though you find there the thread of priesthood, it is a very strange priesthood, the perversion of it.

I see that I had to struggle to come up from that very low level. On the other hand I thank the masters so much that in spite of all of this, Morya never left me. Why else would it be that even as a little child, I rejected the gods of my father? Why else would I never want to have anything to do with the deep practices of that religion, like partaking of the things from the shrine?

I was literally the first person to bring the light of the Christian faith to my family. My eldest brother, Kwame Afram, became a fetish priest, like my father. He used to say that after him I should be the next fetish priest. Even when I was a minister, he would say this. This made me laugh. I never had any thought of doing so.

One time I had a real quarrel with him on this subject. He said to me, "Any time I lead a festival, you are never there."

I laughed. I really laughed.

Then he said, "Why should you laugh at me? There is a church in our village, and even the minister of this church comes to my festival when I invite him. You say you are a minister, and yet you won't attend my festivals."

I laughed again, and I said, "This is the path you have chosen. And I have chosen a different path."

He said, "Ha! So you think that I am a devil! But this is the path, the religion that our ancestors left for us. This is what I have come into. This means that you are rejecting me and your family."

I laughed again. It infuriated him and made him really angry.

I said, "No, I am not laughing at you. But the point is that what you are saying is not the real reason. I have chosen this path and you have chosen that path. Let us agree that we will all move on. We are following different lines, and those lines will never meet. The earlier you accept this, the better for you and for me and for peace in our family."

I laughed so much because of what had been shown me. I had made that inner journey to the temple at Luxor, and I said to my friends there, "You promised you would come for me. But you never came. Now I am back."

They simply said, "Oh, but we were always with you."

God is a great dramatist. The masters placed me in these difficult situations, but they guided me. I feel extremely grateful to Morya that he never left me. I have been through these experiences. I have been where my people are, and to rescue them I had to come up through them, to experience all the things they do.

Chapter 24

Watch and Pray

Walking on the spiritual path and choosing to be with the Brotherhood on that path is always a risk. It is a calculated risk, but it is a risk worth taking.

It is a risk because apart from the external opposition, the most vicious ones are always from within the fold. We have a saying in Ghana that the insects that bite are always from your own towel. It is always so because within the fold there are those who cannot pull their own weight. And they become envious of those within the fold who are making strides.

This sometimes becomes very painful, excruciatingly painful, to the point that it may demoralize or discourage the true seeker. If you find yourself in this situation, at that point you need to turn within and fall back on your own commitment to the Brotherhood of Light. If the commitment is not deep and sincere, you will fall away. But if it is deep and sincere, you will have the courage to move on, because the Brotherhood will never leave you alone—*never*.

I recall from my own work in the field, sometimes when I had difficulties and I would pray, I would go to sleep and I would see Mother with her sword cutting me free. Some of these struggles were with members of the Methodist hierarchy, who were very unhappy that I had left them. Fortunately for them, or fortunately for me, I never spoke disparagingly against the Methodist Church. I always praised the Methodist Church for giving me the opportunity of a Christian education. But because of what they expected from me, because they were grooming me to be a lay president of the conference, it hurt the top hierarchy very much when I left. They didn't want to let me go, they thought they could bring me back. But the Guru cut me free, and as she said, I was not meant to be their minister. In fact if I had been their minister, they would have killed me with black magic. That I know very well.

I remember the Guru said that if you put your all into the master's basket, the master puts his all into yours. When I tendered my resignation from the Methodist Church, I had put my all into the masters' basket. It then became the masters' duty, if they had any job for me, to protect me and ensure that I was able to do that job. So the Guru was always defending me.

I remember during one very difficult situation Mother came to me in a dream to cut me free. There was a struggle between me and my elder brother, the fetish priest. He was very angry with me. I took it lightly, but still it bothered me. It kept coming back. It was a continuous, ongoing struggle. Any time I went to the village, I was aware of it. He wasn't happy about the path I had taken.

I remember one day we were discussing a family issue, and he said, "You know, sometimes I don't consciously fight, but mewuramnon, my masters, the ones I serve, do fight for me. When they see something is going to be detrimental to me, they fight for me, and I am not consciously even aware of it."

So I knew that the problem was not just my brother, but also the forces of his religion that were working through him to attack me. In my dream, after Mother had cut me free from the tentacles of darkness, she said, "Paul, you have struggled so much." She took my hand and drew me out of that situation.

I remember several of these events, and this deepens my

trust and my confidence that no matter what, the Brotherhood will always be there for the rescue.

That is why I smile a lot. Because no matter what anyone else says or does, I know there is one who will not fail, I have one I can always trust. That trust can never be betrayed. I pray that I never betray that trust.

It has been always my fear that I will get to a point where I might betray that trust—either consciously or unconsciously. As we live in this octave and on this planet Earth, we cannot put our chest forward and say, "I AM. I would never betray." Because you never know the moment when you will slip. Pride goeth before the fall. That is always my concern, that I never get into the slippery ground where before you know it, you are down.

Fortunes change quickly on the battlefield. And the danger is always greatest when you think you are standing firm and secure. Then you may be off guard, and the next moment they find the chink in your armor.

I recall one day I was in my auto parts store. I was a lay minister at the time, and I always had my Bible with me, reading it. There was a Muslim man who came in to buy something. He stood on the other side of the counter and looked at me, and he said, "Hey! Any time I come to this shop to buy something, you are reading your Bible. That's very good. But I want to tell you something. If the devil wants to fight you, no matter how strong and how very well prepared you are, if you turn your face from the battle and he gives you a knock, you will fall. So what I want to tell you is this: Never lose your guard. Because no matter how strong you are, if the devil gives you a blow unawares, you will fall down before you get up to fight."

This happened some time in the 1970s, but those words still ring in my mind. I can still recall the man's face and this situation.

This man gave me a great weight of wisdom. Perhaps a master sent him to say that. He did not believe in Christ, but he was the voice of Christ. He did not have a Bible, but he understood Christ's teaching. It was the same message that Jesus gave to Peter: "Watch and pray that you fall not into temptation."

Chapter 25

Leader of the Church

At the end of Summit University Level II, we came back to Camelot. A week before I was due to leave to return to Ghana, Annice Booth called me to her office. She was then the director of Ministry and Outreach. She said, "Mother says you are to go back to Ghana as the director of the group. I know your home is in Kumasi. You do not live in Accra, you are not a Ga (the tribe in the Accra area), but what you should do is spend two weeks in Kumasi and spend two weeks in Accra every month. When you are in Accra the group there should take care of all your expenses and your needs."

So I returned to Ghana in December 1981. The day after I arrived in Ghana, I went to Donkoh's office to see him in his role as chairman of the interim board. I said, "I am back, and Mother told me before she sent me that I should be the director of the Church in Ghana."

He said, "Cheee!" In our language when something goes wrong, we say, "Cheee," which means something has happened that we didn't expect. He was clearly shocked at this news. He had no idea this would happen.

Perhaps he was remembering that he had not treated me very well before I left, keeping me waiting for an hour. Maybe he was worried that I would do something to him, but my mind wasn't there. I was past that stage.

Whenever you inherit a congregation, there are always intrigues. You must be always prepared to handle such things. There are those who owe allegiance to the former leader, so they try to put stumbling blocks in your way. What they should do, they won't; if you give directions, they will not obey.

So initially there were problems. They were in Accra, I was in Kumasi. I was the boss, and they were thinking, "We know Accra and we will see what you will do." They did not say that openly. But I remember the first conference I was responsible for, Easter 1982. I met with the interim board and I said, "We are going to have the Easter conference, so what should we do? What are the programs that we should have?"

I waited one week, we assembled again, and they hadn't done anything. Another week came and went, and they still hadn't done anything.

I had just come from Camelot and been in all the fire and discipline of the Guru-chela relationship there, and I could not take it. I thought, "Headquarters wouldn't tolerate this, Mother wouldn't tolerate this." So I sat down and wrote my own program for the Easter conference. I lined up everything.

When we met the next week, I asked them if they had drawn up the program yet. And they said, "Oh, we need time to do this."

I said, "The Easter conference is coming and I see you are not ready yet, so this is my program. This is what we are going to do at the conference."

One of them said, "No, no, no. That's not how we do things here. We do things by consensus, we all plan together, we do things together."

I said, "Yes, I know. But do you want me to wait until after Easter before we make the program? What will we be celebrating? I saw that you were delaying. And as the director, I am answerable to the messenger and not to you committee members. If anything is going wrong, headquarters will hold the director responsible, not the board. So in the exercise of my function, my duty, I am going ahead. When you are ready to join me, come, there will be space for you. Other than that, I'm moving forward."

From that point I had a half-hearted cooperation. I had to develop very strong feet and hands. Then they realized, this man is a hard man. He wants to go ahead, he wants to ignore us. And I really did ignore their protestations and moved on. Thank God, thanks to the Methodist Church, and thanks to the masters for preparing me for these tests. The masters knew what I had in store and they let me go through all of this in the Methodist Church.

Six months after I arrived back in Ghana, Donkoh left Ghana. He was an accountant, and he signed on with an accounting company and went to work in Kaduna, Nigeria. He had been working with Krakue for many years while I was in Kumasi, and he knew everything about the organization—the files, the papers, everything. So this was a big loss, and I had to figure out everything myself.

When I look back on this time, I also see Mother's foresight and I am grateful for the training she gave me at Summit University. While we were traveling around Montana, we sometimes received mail that had been forwarded from Camelot. In one city, I received an item which was addressed to "Rev. Paul Kyei." One of my classmates saw this and said, "Paul, you are a minister?"

"Yes, I am a minister of this church. I have been a minister since September 1976."

He said, "Ooh! You are a minister. And we have been playing together, doing all sorts of things, and sharing together in love. And we had no clue that you were a minister."

Then the teaching assistant said, "You did not know Paul is

a minister? That's why Mother told me to give him the *hardest* training."

I looked at her, and she realized she had made a mistake. She had revealed her secret instructions. She said, "Oh, sorry, sorry."

I said, "Ah, the cat is out of the bag."

The Guru knew what I would have to do when I returned to Ghana, and I thank God that I had the hardest training. I was ready for the challenges that would come. So when Donkoh left, I said, "No problem."

Later Rev. Gbewonyo also left to go to Nigeria, which meant that both of the lay ministers who were on the interim board left. Paul Lartey, the layman on the board, had withdrawn even before I returned from Camelot. So I had to form a completely new board, and I was now the only minister to work with this group.

I appointed a new secretary, and he has filled that post since then. He found that when he was serving the masters, he had a rapid rise in the civil service of Ghana. Now he is second in charge of his department for the whole country.

I let the members know that I expected them to be serious about the teachings. When a member would come to me with a problem, I would say, "Did you bring your decree book?" If they said "No," I would say, "Well, whatever I'm going to tell you, it will include giving decrees. If you don't have your decree book, what do you want me to do?"

That is the way I tried to help them see that as a Keeper of the Flame, if you have a problem you use the decrees. When you think you have done what you can and you want further help, then you can come to me—but I won't do everything for you.

So I had to console people, but I also had to be a little bit tough here and there. They got to know that I was a no-nonsense director. If they would try to do something that was unacceptable in the church, I would say, "No, this is not acceptable. You can't do this." I set a standard, and they understood.

I also know that you must feed people spiritually, so we used to have a lot of novenas to support them with decrees and we provided a lot of teaching. Each Sunday we would play a new lecture by the messenger and have a discussion about it, and they were interested. You have to feed them. This is how we gradually built the church, how the masters built their church.

Some of those who followed Krakue came back over time. We did not consciously go after them. But when they came back they saw that this was the real teaching, they saw that the tapes of the messengers were played. When they saw the programs that really benefited them, they stayed.

Chapter 26

The White Ray

In my early years in these teachings, I thought that the ray of discipline was the blue ray, the first ray. Later I found out that Mother said that the ray of discipline is the white ray. The fourth ray, whose Chohan is Serapis Bey, is the ray of the disciplinarian. It seems that I serve on the white ray.

Most people know that the white ray is the ray of purity. I see the white ray as also the ray of transparency. This transparency extends to all aspects of relationships. In that ray you cannot consciously or deliberately hide anything. If you walk in the white ray, everyone must see what is, as well as seeing what she or he has also to do to come up higher.

As human beings living here on planet earth, there cannot be transparency all the way through. But transparency also includes the point of acceptance of error and mistakes. When we think of it in that way, it is easy to admit when there is an error and it is also quite easy to say, "I am sorry, let's forgive and move on." No matter what ray an individual serves on, if we will all turn to the ray of purity with all it entails, life will be better lived.

When we want to describe the light of God, we speak of the white light. In this teaching we go to the extent of explaining that white does not denote race or discrimination but the white light of God. The white light is integral to creation itself. There was void over the face of the earth and God said, "Let there be light," and there was light.

Consciously or unconsciously, whether people are on the path or not, everyone loves the color white—and this is true even in everyday life. For example, when someone loses a relative, people wear black as a sign of mourning. In our culture a woman will wear black for one full year after the death of her husband. At the end of this year there is a ceremony, a little service. Friends are invited and it is made public that she is putting off the black and putting on the white, which signifies that the period of mourning and sorrow is over. So when someone is happy, he puts on white. The white light and the purity flame also engender happiness and joy.

When I first assumed the responsibility for the church in Ghana, I looked at the members and the response that I received from them was not what I had hoped for. They seemed to be shying away from me.

One Sunday, I noticed one of the members at church, and as I looked at him I sensed that he had a problem. So I called him, "Ernest, come. Would you like to talk to me?"

He bowed his head, he was looking at the ground. He didn't say anything. So I said, "Please, can you come and see me on Tuesday in the office?" Reluctantly, he agreed.

That Tuesday when we met, I said to him, "I felt that you needed someone to talk to, that you had a problem."

He said, "Reverend, to be honest with you I did not want to talk to you, even though I knew that I needed to talk to you about my problem. And I am not the only one. We think you are too strict, too hard a disciplinarian."

Then he asked me, "Don't you see that we are all shying away from you? It's not that we don't like you. We like you, but we think that you are too much of a disciplinarian."

I said, "I didn't know. Maybe if you had told me earlier,

things would have changed a little."

Then I said, "But the problem is that Mother spent her money, the church's money, and sent me all over America to train me, and she gave me the responsibility to head this church. I owe a duty to her and the Brotherhood to ensure that this church moves on.

"Did you know that when the former Bishop was removed, the church was shaky? Things were not right with the organization, and after he left, some people wanted to follow him out. He was a compromiser, and they thought that I would follow that path. So I needed to be strong and have a strong hand for discipline. If they find me too strict, that is because it is a new field I am charting and I needed to chart it very well.

"But I love everyone. Because without the people there cannot be a church. Tell your friends that I am the best friend they could have."

So I came face to face with someone who thought I wanted too much discipline—perhaps to the discomfort of those who were around me. After I explained to him that I wasn't strict to the extent of not caring for people, that I cared for each one, he didn't become a "friend," so to speak. But his attitude was okay, he was more active in the church. I also altered my approach slightly.

For example, it used to be that if someone would come to me to complain about something someone else had done, I would say, "Okay, I will call the person." I would have them both in the room together. "Would you tell me in his presence what you told me?" That was my way of dealing with gossip. It stopped them from coming to me to talk about other members of the church. But some of them didn't like the way I did it.

Now, if someone comes to me with a situation like this, instead of immediately calling the other person in, I will listen to what they have come to tell me. I will not act immediately on it. I will let some days pass, try to see whether I will need to see the other individual and talk to him or her privately about the issue. I try to be more diplomatic, rather than the direct way of doing things.

At the same time, without discipline there would be chaos. It is because of discipline that we have laws and regulations in society. If everyone were to take to his or her own way of doing what he thinks he should do, there would be chaos. So there must be discipline to regulate conduct. That's what I think.

Mother taught that in starting a new movement there has to be a very tight spiral of discipline and order. Gradually with time it will loosen, but if you don't have it tight at the beginning, by the end it will be very loose and the dispensation can be lost.

Chapter 27

The Weight of the Mantle

When I first arrived at Camelot in 1981, I was looking for Mother. I wanted to meet her and tell her I had arrived. She used to live there at that time, right on the campus. I went to the building where she lived and I told her secretary that I wanted to see her. The secretary said I could not.

So there we were: I was pleading with the secretary, and she *wasn't* going to allow me to see Mother. She was even trying to tell me that Mother wasn't around. Then suddenly I saw Mother coming from upstairs. I turned round to look at her, and this girl looked at me. The lid had been blown off her story.

When Mother came down the stairs, she came over to me and held both of my hands in hers. Usually when Mother met me, she would hug me. But this time she stretched out her hands to hold mine and she pulled me into her office, which was on the other side of the entrance hall.

She asked me about six questions in a row. I was just looking at her, wondering which one to answer.

Then she said, "You know, I am going through an initiation with Saint Germain. That's why I couldn't hug you." That was not long after Saint Germain had helped Mother to balance the remaining portion of her karma. She told me it was not safe for her to be in close contact with anyone. Whether it was not safe in relation to herself or the other person, I dared not ask.

Then she sat me down and said, "Herbert Krakue was engaged in mental malpractice—trying to suppress everyone else with his knowledge." He did not want anyone else to rise up. And I believed that, because I had seen him try to do this to me.

"But you know, Paul, if I had not done what I did to Krakue, if I had not defrocked him as Bishop of Africa, you would not have been able to come here the second time." I do not know why this was so. Mother did not explain further.

She continued, "What the masters do is that when the person who should hold a certain position is not ready, they place someone else there until the rightful person matures to that stage where he can hold the office, and then they restore him to it."

I almost can't describe my reaction. Was I surprised? For the understanding dawned on me at once that what Krakue feared was true. Somehow he felt within himself that I would be the one to take his place, and it was so. That was the revelation that the Guru gave me, even though I did not yet know what it would mean to be "ready" or when that would occur.

Events proved that Herbert was only a caretaker or a place-holder for a while. It is clear now that the master was waiting for the ancient mantle to be restored, which was revealed to me in that great ceremony that I witnessed when I was at the Inner Retreat twenty years after this.

I was so happy to hear this revelation from Mother. But I must say that I was also a little frightened. I do not know exactly what frightened me, but perhaps even then I had some sense of what the ancient mantle would bring with it, its weight, which I experienced even physically when I had the vestment made and wore it. Perhaps I also had some sense of having lost the mantle in the past and what it cost me to fail at that time.

Even though Krakue was a placeholder, his soul also had opportunity. At any time he could have chosen to bend the knee and pass his tests, either before or after he held the office. But he messed things up very badly. And of all those who were made lay ministers on his recommendation, only Kobina Donkoh, Grant Gbewonyo and Appoh, an old man, remained. The rest all disappeared. They were all made lay ministers, and when Krakue was gone, they all left.

People have asked me, "Morya commissioned Krakue as bishop, and Mother made all these people lay ministers, and yet they left. Did Mother know this would happen? Did Morya know?"

I cannot answer for Mother. I can only explain the circumstances through which these people were brought to her to be made ministers.

From the beginning, because of all the leadership experience I had in the Methodist Church, Krakue was afraid that I would take over his office. When Mother consecrated him as the Bishop of Africa and then the very next day made me a lay minister, I think he felt his fears were beginning to materialize.

He protested to Mother about me being made a minister. When he found out that my appointment was at Morya's command, he could not argue with that. So he said, "Okay, I have no ministers in Accra. Why don't you appoint some lay ministers here?"

Mother said, "I do not have any instruction from the masters as to who they should be. You are here and you know the people. Give me your recommendations." Krakue wrote a list of about twenty people who he wanted as lay ministers. They were his friends, men and women of substance. Mother made some of them lay ministers.

The first problem was that most of them were not inclined for the ministry. They were made ministers because Krakue wanted them. He had no indication that they had the desire to be ministers or the aptitude for the ministry.

133

Secondly, he felt that if I was the only other minister in Ghana, it would be seen that I would in the natural course of things be his successor. But I was in Kumasi, and he was in Accra, and if he could have these other ministers in Accra, they would be like a hedge around him to prevent me from coming in. So the motive by which he called them was not sound.

Beyond that, many of these lay ministers were tied to Krakue rather than the masters, the mission, the messenger. You find that this is the case in many organizations. If the leader is not selfless, he creates a situation where people who are elevated to a certain position in the organization owe their appointment to him. If they don't do his bidding, they feel they may fall out of favor and lose the positions they hold. They won't say anything, even if what the leader is doing is not right.

It also becomes a paramount interest to such appointees to ensure that the leader stays. If he stays, then their position is guaranteed. If he leaves, their position is lost. This becomes a personality cult.

As you study human character and behavior, you find that some of the people appointed in this way will actually receive the light and the truth and they will begin to follow the light and the truth. After a period of time, they will become dis-enchanted with the leadership. They will dare to stand firm, and the relationship between them and the leader is broken. In that situation, when the leader is removed, they remain to defend the truth upon which the organization was founded—as Donkoh, Gbewonyo and Appoh did.

Those who are not tied to a higher cause, but only to the one who is giving favors, will often leave if that one leaves. The whole structure is based on favoritism, so it does not have a good grounding. When the leader is swept away, the followers don't have any sound foundation and they waver. They cannot even fulfill the requirements of the offices they hold. The honest ones will pull out. The others will not fulfill their duties, so they will have to be shown the way out. That's what happens.

Such a system will crumble—unless you have people who are strong, people who believe in the mandate of the organization and decide to uphold it.

Like Krakue, these lay ministers all had their tests and their opportunities. Whether Morya knew what the outcome would be, I do not know. But the masters have often said that even if the likelihood of failure is high for a particular individual, they do not hold this as their vision. They place their attention on the victory and seek to help each soul to reach that goal.

Chapter 28

Two Pillars

Reverend Kobina Donkoh was my friend. He has passed on now, but I don't think he would mind my sharing this story of his life and our work together.

When I returned to Ghana from Camelot, Donkoh did not openly voice any unhappiness about my being made the director, apart from the initial shock when he heard this. His reaction was to leave the country and go to Nigeria, and I think that did him some good, because he had time to reflect. After twelve years, he came back a changed person. Some other things also helped to build our relationship.

In 1985 I took on his daughter, Nada, to be my secretary. Nada was about twenty at that time, and I cared for her as my daughter. I really extended a fatherly concern for her. When he saw this, I think it helped Donkoh to see that Kyei is probably a good man.

The second thing was what happened when his son died. It was sudden and unexpected. Donkoh was in Nigeria and his son was in Ghana. His son was a welder and he was working on a car. It started raining so he stopped welding and switched off the electricity. After the rain had stopped, he wanted to continue what he was doing, so he switched on the electricity and went under the car. They don't know exactly what happened, but he was electrocuted. It was so sudden and he died

Rev. Kobina Donkoh

straight away. This was very painful for Donkoh. It was his only son.

Donkoh came back to Ghana. I stood by him, I helped. I spent a lot of time with him, trying to comfort him. I remember at the cemetery, he nearly collapsed. The pain was too much for him. I was so close and holding him and comforting him. So he realized I was very generous and I was there to uphold him. I did not tell him this, and perhaps he did not know, but I very much appreciated who he was. Donkoh was in the teachings many years before me. When I first registered and I came from Kumasi to attend my first meeting of The Summit Lighthouse in Accra, Donkoh was the first person I met. He received me with love, with joy that a new person had come in. The way he received me created a very good impression and I think, along with my own inner preparation, really encouraged me to stay with these teachings.

The other thing that helped Donkoh with his perception of me was that when he returned to Ghana, he saw the church was growing. He saw a great joy and great improvement compared to when he left. He saw the great forward movement of the church. I remember at one of the meetings we made an appeal for funds, and the response was so good it really baffled him. And he said, "During the time of the former Bishop, he would make appeals but they would not get that response." So all of these points together, I think, helped him to realize that we needed to pull together and get things moving.

In 1996, after I had been the director of the church in Ghana for fourteen years, Donkoh was made the director. I handed over to him happily.

When he took over, one thing Donkoh changed was to stop the public outreach we had been doing. He thought it was a waste of time and money because we did not have many people coming into the teachings as a result. I felt this was a short-sighted decision, but Donkoh was the head of the church, the director, and I did not want to create the appearance of any controversy or disagreement between us. So I simply said okay. I packed all my lecture notes, tapes, and everything I used for outreach and sent them all to Kumasi, which is my home base. I really wanted to retire and sit in my own home.

After the outreach had been stopped for about a year or so, the members started asking why this was done. They thought that because I was no longer the director of the church, I did not want to do it anymore. When they learned that it wasn't my decision but rather a policy of the director, they started pressuring Donkoh to restart the program.

After this had gone on for quite a time, Donkoh came to see me one time I was visiting Accra, asking me to help with outreach again. I told him that because of the decision he had made, I withdrew and I had even switched off my mind from even thinking about public outreach and other things that we used to do.

Then he told me he had received a dream that there should be two pillars in the church to help its growth. He saw that I held the Alpha flame and he held the Omega flame, and we should pull together to help the church grow. Then he said, "So please, I'm begging you to stay strong and let's cooperate and build together." And he was genuine. I still recall where he sat in my sitting room in my home in Accra. He sat close by and he talked. I just watched and listened as he spoke.

Then I said, "For fourteen years the masters used me to build up the church. At the time I took over, Krakue was hanging around and trying to run his own organization. But we stood firm and built the church. You went away. You came back and saw the progress that we had made. You saw the church stronger than when you left it. When you became the director, you wanted to do things your own way and it seemed that you did not want my help. So I had to give you an opportunity. I had served my term, now it was your turn, and I didn't want to interfere with what you were trying to do.

"If you would like us now to work together, I will be very willing to help. If there was any problem between us, it is over. If you want to do outreach again and you are willing to spend the money for hiring the hall, well, I have a commission from the messenger and I cannot refuse to carry out that commission."

So I went back to Kumasi and brought my notes and out-reach materials back to Accra, and we started all over again. I opened my heart and we worked together. From that time on, there was no major decision he would take as the director without consulting me. I always shared my ideas with him. So we really worked together, and in 2001, when I was made the regional minister, he became my right-hand man, my chief consultant. The cooperation became even greater so that we could move the church onward.

I think Donkoh found the teachings in 1964. A year later the center in Accra was recognized and given a certificate. Mark Prophet called it the first Summit Lighthouse church in Africa, and Donkoh had been a great pillar in the church since that time. During the period of Krakue's leadership, and after I had replaced Krakue, he stood there. We worked together. When the ministerial training program was set up in Africa in the 1990s, he was very instrumental in its success.

I looked at his service, his contributions over the years, and

Rev. Kyei and Rev. Donkoh in 2009

I felt that he should be ordained as a minister (he was still a lay minister). I was the only ordained minister in Africa at that time, and I thought we needed more, and he was worthy. So in 2005 I wrote a petition to the Ministerial Council recommending Donkoh be ordained, and they agreed. They asked him to come to the Inner Retreat for his ordination. I went to the Inner Retreat with him for the July conference in 2005. It was his first and only visit to the Inner Retreat, and he was the only one ordained at that conference.

The two of us were then the only ordained ministers in this church in Africa, and we remained so until Donkoh died in July 2010. He was seventy-three.

So we are now back to one ordained minister in Africa. I am looking forward to the newly commissioned lay ministers in Africa also rising up to be ordained.

Chapter 29

Black Magic

You can't be a minister in Africa without coming into contact with black magic. People who practice it are all around, and I have come across it many times in my years of service. Here are a few of those incidents.

At the time I was made a minister, in 1976, I had a cousin who was very close, like a sister to me. One of her closest friends, also a cousin, came to me to warn me about her, "Watch your sister very, very carefully. Keep yourself away from her."

I said, "But she is my sister."

She said, "If you knew what your sister has been planning for you, you would put miles and miles and miles between the two of you."

I said, "Is that so? Well, I don't know. I think if it is needed God will double the miles between us so that she will not catch up with me." And I prayed that God would keep me safe.

I don't know why they were doing this, but I think this cousin and her friends had been practicing witchcraft and they had planned that they would make a kebab of me for Christmas. That's what they had planned at their witches meeting, that she would use witchcraft to kill me.

I always pray for my protection, the protection of my family, my wife and children, the protection of my community, the church members, the protection of the lightbearers. That's my prime concern. And so if the witches would like to have a meeting over me, that's their business. And I think Archangel Michael fought a good fight for me in this situation. It's amazing. This cousin professed to be a Catholic. One day she went to the early mass, and she stood up to pray in the church and she collapsed. They sent her to the hospital, and that was all. She was dead.

The cousin who had warned me about her, hearing about this, came to me when I went to the village and said, "Your God is a strong God. He fought for you."

I said, "Archangel Michael took care of it. He sent back to her what she had tried to send to me."

One time in 1985 I visited Lagos, Nigeria. I lodged in a guest house belonging to someone I knew there. Apart from the main building, there was a separate place which was the family apartment, and I had a guest room there.

There was a verandah outside my room, and I brought a seat outside and I sat there for a long time before I went back into my room to sleep. I did not know anything about what the wife of the owner was doing in her room, but I think she had a male friend who was visiting her there.

Apparently this man took offense that I stayed there for a very long time, preventing him from coming out of this woman's room. And he was a black magician, otherwise he would not do what he did. That night I woke up feeling something like a needle in my spine, between my shoulder blades. It was serious.

I have a practice that wherever I go, I take a wallet-sized chart of the divine self and I put it on the table in my room, rest it against something to stand it up, and it becomes my altar. I got out of bed and went to this altar. I decreed from 1 a.m. until 5 a.m., reversing the tide. The pain went away. I felt relieved. Everything was okay.

That very day I was due to return to Ghana. In the afternoon, around two o'clock, I came down to the office to say goodbye to the wife of the owner of the guest house. I opened the office door, and there was the man who had been with her that night. The moment he saw me, he fell flat on his face.

I looked at him. At once it registered in my mind that he was the one who had attacked me that night. I stood there watching him, and the lady sat in her seat, also watching him. The man was lying prostrate, flat on the floor. I stood there for what seemed to be about fifteen minutes. The woman could not speak. She just looked at me and looked at the man lying on the floor.

Then I said, "I have come to say goodbye. I am going back home to Ghana. Thank you very, very much for your hospitality." So I said goodbye to her and left.

This man thought he had killed me. He was shocked to see me still alive. And the energy he sent out could not perform its function, so by law it had to return to him. That was what had happened.

Later that year, Mother went on a European stump. I went to London to see her. From London we were all going to travel to Flevehof, in Holland, where Mother was holding a seminar.

When I got to London, I stayed with a cousin. Her husband's daughter was not a good girl, and she apparently did not like my presence in the home. One evening we were watching a television program and she offered to make tea. I felt that she might put something in the tea, so I said to her, "Oh, don't worry." But she made the tea anyway, and I drank it. After a while I felt very uncomfortable, so I went to my room and made my calls, many calls, and decreed for some hours before I went to sleep.

The following day we were all leaving to go to Holland.

I got up in the morning and got myself ready. When I came from my room, this girl saw me. She ran straight back to her room. She was frightened, because I was still alive.

I came back about a week later, after the seminar. I asked my cousin, "Where is your stepdaughter?"

She said, "The morning you left, she left the house and never returned again."

Sometimes black magic manifests in very strange ways. Recently I went to my village, and there was an incident there involving a widow and her children. We knew that this woman had been playing with these dark practices. The children, particularly the two sons, felt they were having difficulty in life because of this. They attend a church where the pastor says that he deals with such things. They brought this man to their house, and he said he would remove the witchcraft that was there. He asked for one goat and $500.

First he had to pacify the woman. They went to her house, she pointed to a certain place. They tried to dig, and they said the thing they were trying to find was running under the ground. They dug at three different places, and finally, they got it. The pastor tried to bring it out from the hole they had dug. It shook him, it kicked him like an electric shock. Finally he was able to put his hand in the hole and brought out an earthenware pot.

When they tried to open this pot, they were amazed to find that they could not break it. Finally, they tried shooting it with a gun. They fired three bullets at it before the pot broke. Inside there was a mixture of many different things, including human blood and some cowrie shells. They set a fire and burned them all and threw the ashes into the toilet.

Such events are not unusual in Africa. I don't know if this is true in other nations, but in much of Africa people are really frightened by black magicians and their witchcraft. They are so scared.

I still recall the face of one of the Keepers of the Flame who I met in the Congo in 2011. After our seminar there, we had an opportunity for people to ask questions. This man was so concerned with black magic and witchcraft practiced against him. He talked about what he feared in his own workplace, then about his family. He said that his wife was a trader and she thought that someone was using this juju to make sure that she didn't prosper, was not successful in her trade. He asked if it is good to pray for her.

I said, "She is your wife, you are karmically tied to her. She has interests in your fortune as much as you have interests in hers. So if you're praying for your protection, then you really have to pray for the protection of your wife and whatever she is doing."

He said he didn't know if it was right to do so.

I said, "Why not? It's right to pray for her."

He said, "Okay. Can I teach her any of the decrees? Since she is not a Keeper of the Flame, is it right for her to recite the decrees?"

I said, "Of course. It's a prayer, you can teach her."

So he said, "Okay. Show me what are the decrees I have to teach her so that the forces of black magic and witchcraft preventing people from buying from her will cease, they won't worry her again. I'll use them for myself too, so I can also be successful."

This taught me a great deal. Everywhere you go it's the same on the African continent. There is great fear of witchcraft and black magic, and people are really yearning to be free of it and to know how to protect themselves.

The practice of witchcraft in Africa, and I think by extension in the Caribbean and other areas, is not child's play. This is real, and those who indulge in it can make life miserable for those who do not have the Science of the Spoken Word—which is the antidote to all of it. So people need to be taught continuously how to defend against it using the spiritual tools that we have. The African traditional doctors claim that they help the people free themselves from the activities of the witch doctors and their black magic. They can provide only a temporary cure, at best. But when people find the teachings of the masters, those who are really serious and give the decrees see that they can gain their freedom.

As I travel around Africa, I find that black magic and witchcraft varies in intensity, and so does the level of people's belief. In some places their belief is so deep, it is to the point where people are terrorized by it. In Ghana, however, even though the belief is there, it is not so pronounced compared to other African nations where I have been.

I believe this is because the masters' teachings have been there and the decrees have been going on since March 1964, when The Summit Lighthouse was founded in Accra. So all this number of years, these decrees continuing have certainly done something to improve the entire national environment.

Another difference in Ghana is that we have ministers of our church there. I am there, Rev. Donkoh was there, Rev. Gbewonyo is there, as well as all the more recent lay ministers. People have someone to go to if they are worried about black magic. We make our calls and we also teach them how to make their own calls.

Every Sunday after the Sacred Ritual and the announcements, we have decrees. After that we give everyone in the congregation the opportunity to come to the altar, row by row. They kneel in front of the statue of Mother Mary from the grotto erected near the altar in the sanctuary. We give them time while we play recordings of Mother's invocations. They give their own prayers, whatever is their need of the hour, whatever has been a sore point in their life during the week. It helps them, and they love it.

We try to bring little innovations to the service to make them happy, so that they feel they are a part of the service. And they need these teachings all the time.

But I see that in the absence of a minister, they would miss so much. In Africa the minister is a unifying force. People have great love for the minister and great respect.

Chapter 30

The Wisdom of the Mother

In the 1980s, I used to hold public lectures. Every three months we had a public lecture in Accra, and we rotated to different locations around the city. At one of these lectures there was a man who was the host of a television program on Ghana Television, the national station run by the government.

He told me later that what amazed him about our event was that my lecture started on time. He wondered, "How is it that this man said two o'clock and at two o'clock he is on the podium giving the lecture?" He had never attended any function that started on time.

It's a habit in Africa—I think it's even a disease, a chronic one—that things do not start on time. We have a joke, we say "African time." You hardly ever have a function that starts on time. When they say three o'clock, you are sure it will start around four, sometimes even five. But we have made it a point that with our lectures in this church, when we say it is three, we start at three. Even if there is only one person there, we will start at three.

On this day, I was at the podium at five minutes to two. At exactly two o'clock, I stood up. "Please stand. Let us pray."

When this man saw that I did this, he said to himself, "I must approach this man. He must have something really good." He arranged to meet me, he interviewed me, and he asked me to appear on his program as one of the panelists. That's how we started on television in Ghana.

The program was called *Contemplation,* and it focused on religious issues. We prerecorded the program during the week and it aired on Sunday evening. There were ministers from a number of different congregations on the show, and I was a primary member for many months.

This program really helped douse the hostility that the politicians and the university personnel generated against Mother when she visited in 1978. At that time the people did not really know, or care to know, the message of our Guru. But with this program, many people got to know that she really had something wonderful for them, and that it was those who had their own agendas who had prevented the masses from listening when she was in Ghana.

However, there was a lot of opposition to this program from some quarters. We would be very straightforward with people. We let them know that the power, God, the Christ, is within them. And the mainline churches didn't like it. They claimed that we were giving a teaching that was making rebels out of their members. They thought that the masters' teaching was giving too much freedom to the people, because it let them know what they could do to be real Christians, if they wanted to.

I understand there was wrangling on the board of the Ghana Broadcasting Corporation, the government body that ran GTV. There was one lady on the board who was really opposed to the program and said the program should be taken off the air.

I think the opposition was focused on Rev. Kyei being there. There were those who knew me as Mr. P. K. Kyei, youth worker of the Methodist Church. Now this man is on Ghana Television, on national television, and he says he is a reverend.

He has metamorphosed into a minister who is giving a teaching that is quite strange.

So they tried asking, "Where did he train? How did he become a minister?" Unfortunately, they miscalculated. I told them, "Well, I was trained here, I went for a course here ..." I listed all of my training and qualifications. That put a stop to that line of argument—but the opposition continued.

I happen to have a friend on the GTV board who narrated all of this to me. We laughed about it. I said, "Well, if I come on the radio or on the television and you don't like what I'm saying, then turn off your radio or television. But don't prevent others from listening."

They even tried to dictate the panelists who should serve on the program. However, the man who was doing the program wasn't in a mood to entertain that kind of thing. He preferred to withdraw rather than allow himself to be manipulated in this way.

After I had been on the program about a year, another person took over. He renamed the show *About Life*. Even more than before he called in to the show those who belonged to esoteric movements, because he knew that the esoteric teachings were different from what is given forth to the people from the pulpits of the orthodox and mainline churches. There was a moderator and two panelists, and he had Buddhists, Krishnas, Rosicrucians, many different people on the show.

The strange thing was that there was never a Muslim on the panel. I don't know if the Muslims refused to sit on it, but I don't remember having a Muslim on the panel the whole time we were there.

It was a discussion program. The moderator would bring the questions, put a topic on the table, and ask us to discuss it and give our views. I would always say, "This is what the masters say on this particular subject," and share that perspective. This was often quite different from what the orthodox people would say on any given subject, and this made it quite interesting and appealing to the people.

I remember once there was a Catholic priest on the show. He is now the Bishop in Accra. We were talking about evil. I told him, "*Evil* is *live* spelled backward. L-i-v-e, you take it from the other end, it is e-v-i-l."

This priest said, "Yes, we are all learning here."

The head of the station got so interested in our discussions that he instructed his personal secretary to ask me to record a series of short segments that would air each evening on GTV before the station closed, a prayer or a short talk on the masters' teachings.

This man arranged all the equipment and the crew to record these segments. Either fortunately or unfortunately, that was the day they were having the memorial service for Samora Machel, the late president of Mozambique. So the TV crew went to record that instead. The head of the station was not a religiously inclined person generally, so people thought that he would be more interested in having the recording of the politicians than a religious program, but I understand he was very cross with them that they did not record the sessions with me.

That was how we missed the golden opportunity to give the masters' teachings every evening on GTV as the last prayer before the station closes down. As far as I know, they did not come looking for me again to record these segments. That was really an opportunity missed. GTV is the only station that covers all of the country. Later on we had our own shows on private TV stations, but they don't have the wide coverage of GTV.

Contemplation and *About Life* covered many different issues from all points of view. The host of *Contemplation* once said he was amazed to hear me speak about all these subjects. He said, "In your church, you seem to talk about every religious subject. And when I ask you questions, you do not hesitate—everything flows, it just comes out. How do you do it?"

I smiled and I said, "It's the wisdom of the Mother." That was all the answer I gave him.

As for me, as a person alone, I don't know anything. But the answers flow when you ask, because it is the truth. It is the wisdom of the Mother.

Chapter 31

The Church's Role in Difficult Times

Before I left Camelot after finishing Summit University Level II, Mother held a reception for the students, a luncheon in her house for our group. I remember she sat at the end of the table.

After talking to each of us, she said, "Some of you are going to experience some very unpleasant events in your countries." She did not name the countries. I arrived back in Ghana at the end of December 1981. Exactly one week after I returned, there was another military coup, the second by Jerry John Rawlings. I remembered then what the Guru had said, and I realized that her prophecy had come true.

It was a dangerous time in Ghana. Where I lived in Accra was quite close to the studios of the Ghana Broadcasting Corporation, and I woke up one morning to find a spent cartridge in front of my garage. If the shooting had been in the daytime, someone could have died.

Ghana was under the rule of Rawlings and his military regime for the next eleven years, and it was a time of trouble. Political parties were outlawed. The media was silenced, and criticism of the government or its program of left-wing revolution was suppressed. Public tribunals were set up to try those accused of "anti-government" actions. Some opponents of the government were even tortured, murdered or imprisoned without trial. There are still some two hundred people who are not accounted for.

At one of our conferences we were playing the dictations and lectures from the Class of the Elohim. In one of those lectures, Mother really lashed out at the communists—Castro, Ortega, Gadhafi. Some Keepers of the Flame in Ghana did not like that, and I think they reported me to the military. One of the Keepers who did that came back to me and said, "I have been asked to warn you."

I said, "Who asked you to warn me?"

She said, "You know them, these people."

I said, "What are they saying?"

"They said you are getting involved in politics in the church and I must warn you."

I said, "Is that all? Go and tell them that I'm not afraid of them, not for one farthing."

She said, "Director? You want me to tell them this?

And I said, "Yes, that is what I am saying. Go and tell them I am not afraid of them—not for one farthing. The tape we are playing is not my words. It is the words the messenger, our Guru, has told us, and I'm playing this for all of you to hear. If at any point these people don't like what I'm saying, it is their business, not my business. Whatever they want to be their reaction to what I'm saying is their business also, not mine. My business is to give out the masters' teaching. If they do not like it, that is their business. It is not my business."

And she said, "What if these military people, if someone enters the room and shoots you?"

I said, "It's no problem. The one coming in to shoot me, it is his problem. My problem is to give the masters' teaching. If he doesn't like it and he takes out a weapon and comes and shoots me, that is his business, not mine."

She looked at me and said, "All right."

And I said, "Good, you can go."

Looking back, I see that I did not have a shred of fear of the military when I was saying those things. I really did not fear them. Firstly, I was prepared for anything. Secondly, I was convinced that the path they had taken by pursuing socialism and communism was not the right thing for our country.

In a different situation, I might handle it differently, but this is what I felt I should do in that circumstance. I think the masters will always give us the direction we need—in any situation, you get the guidance as to how to handle it. I believe that. What I did was the need of the hour. The military were trying to suppress everyone at that time.

After this they did start investigating our church—and me in particular. They did not come to me, but they tried to go through other members of staff in the church. It was not done openly, but behind the scenes. It was all designed to make us cower down.

In 1989 they went to the extent of setting up a government committee to investigate all the churches in Ghana. It was called the Religious Affairs Committee. The state wanted to interfere with the way the churches were being run. Churches had to register with the committee and receive approval from them, otherwise they could be closed down and all their property confiscated by the government. They drew up a program and invited all the churches in the country to appear before that committee. In this case, I do give credit to the Christian Council of Ghana—they refused to register. With us and other smaller churches, they could try to intimidate us.

The first step was that a certain lady came to me and said, "Reverend, if you are having any problem with the committee, don't worry. I can intercede for you."

I said, "You can intercede with who? Rawlings? The chairman of the committee? Or who? Thank you very much,

I don't need anyone's intervention." That was the first hostile response I gave.

Whether the committee was scared of me or not, I can't tell, but we happened to be almost the last church to be invited to meet with them. I went with Rev. Gbewonyo. We got to their meeting place and their assistant announced that Rev. Kyei from Church Universal and Triumphant was waiting. It took almost one hour after being announced for us to be invited into the room. I think they had a problem. They did not know who should chair the meeting and ask me the questions. They had a chairman, but he apparently did not want to do it. Eventually a university lecturer who was serving on the committee was chosen to chair the meeting and the substantive chairman sat aside. So I went in with Rev. Gbewonyo.

The first question was, "So, you are from Church Universal and Triumphant."

"Yes."

"From Prophetess Clare."

I said, "No, no, no. Her name is Elizabeth Clare Prophet. Prophet is her name. It is not a title she has assumed."

He said, "Okay."

That was the first faulty statement they made, and I corrected the chairman.

The next question was this: "Your church, how is it governed? Is the leadership elected?"

I replied, "The government of Church Universal and Triumphant follows a theocratic form."

There was an Ahmadiyya Muslim man on the committee, and he said, "Theocratic? Theocratic? What does that mean?"

Then the university lecturer who was presiding over the meeting said, "Oh, it means that the government of their church receives its authority direct from God, and not from men."

I said, "Yes. That's right. Our messenger is appointed by the ascended masters and she derives her authority from what the masters say. So we don't hold elections to elect our messenger."

The Muslim representative said, "Then your Church is not democratic at all."

And I shot back, "How can you, a Muslim, sit here and pass a value judgment on a Christian organization? How can the government do that? You are trying to stifle the churches."

And he said, "No, it's not the government. Don't bring the government into this."

I said, "How is that? You are not here on your own. You are appointed by the government, so if there is any responsibility, the appointing authority has to take it. You are acting for and on behalf of the government. And you are saying that my religion, my church is not democratic. So when you say this to me, in a sense the government is saying it to me.

"If you don't elect your leaders, that doesn't mean you are not democratic. The Roman Catholic Church does not hold elections. But you can't say that, well, the Catholic Church is not democratic. I think that assumption is wrong.

"Let me ask you this question: Do you Muslims go to a meeting and cast your votes to elect your head, your imam or whatever you call him? I have been in this country since the beginning of my life, and I have never seen or heard of you Muslims going to a meeting to elect your leader. The one who leads you is always there because he is appointed by your head in Pakistan."

So the university lecturer said, "No, no, no. We don't want to argue with you on this issue, please. Let's drop it." So they dropped that question.

Then they said, "Okay, Clare Prophet came here to Ghana and spoke about Union Government. She was trying to interfere with the running of our country."

I said, "Well, I don't know what you mean by interference.

Elizabeth Clare Prophet is the messenger of the Great White Brotherhood. She has a branch of her church here and the church is made up of people. You, the government, are concerned with making laws and rules for the welfare of the people. The messenger, or for that matter any religious leader, is also concerned with the people, because the church is made up of people. So you could say that the government and the church are running towards the same goal, the same purpose, which is the welfare of the people.

"Elizabeth Clare Prophet's church has members who are Ghanaians, of which I am one. And so she has concern for us, the members, as the government has concerns for the population. So if Elizabeth Clare Prophet speaks about anything that affects the people, it is her right to do so."

"Okay, okay, okay. We don't want to argue with you on this issue."

It was a very great drama. Anything they said, I gave a reply which threw the question back to them. They would say, "Okay, we don't want to argue with you on this issue."

So we went back and forth like that for almost an hour.

Eventually they said, "You may go. If we need you we will call you again."

And that was all.

Fortunately, or unfortunately, after our appearance the committee was dissolved. I think it was their judgment. I am amazed at my own courage at that time, but that's exactly what I did.

I believe that our ministers must have the courage to defend the masters and their teaching. I found out that when you do that, the opponents back off, they get scared and they pull away. And when you are defending truth you have the support of the masters.

Many years ago, when I was the youth leader in the

Methodist Church, we invited a learned preacher who held a doctorate degree in divinity to speak to the youth group. His name was Rev. Agdeti. He was asked a question about the duty of a Christian under a totalitarian government, and he said, "The best way for a Christian to show his loyalty to a totalitarian government is by disobeying unjust laws."

It sounded beautiful in my ears, but I found it a little awkward. It sounded so odd. How do you show loyalty by disobeying?

And he said, "When you realize that these laws are not for the good of the nation, you show your defense of your nation, your loyalty to your nation, by disobeying that law and doing that which you think is right."

We laughed. We said, "But if you disobey these laws, they will arrest you."

He said, "Yes. But by disobeying that law, breaking that law, it will drive home to them that the law was not right."*

That was quite a revolutionary thought for us. But as young men, we just laughed about it, and I think most of us did not think about it much more. But it really stuck in my mind. And that is what came out when I appeared before the Religious Affairs Committee.

The other side of the question is that if this is the general law of the state and you disobey it, will you not open yourself to persecution or sanctions? How will that limit your mission in this life?

I also think of Jesus' words in the Gospel of Mark, "Render unto Caesar the things that are Caesar's and to God the things

---

* One noted proponent of this philosophy was Mohandas Gandhi, who combined the principles of civil disobedience with *ahimsa* (non-violence and compassion for all life) to secure a peaceful transition to independence for India. Civil disobedience based on principle is very different from breaking a law simply for the purpose of self-gain or self-gratification. In the latter, the individual seeks to avoid punishment. In the former, the individual is willing to face the legal consequences of his actions.

that are God's." Jesus has also told us, through his messenger, that we should obey the laws of the nations, even if those laws are unjust, and that if we seek to change them it should be within the framework provided by the structure of government. The one point of the law that he called us to defend was the right to practice our religion free from persecution and the right to spread the teachings of the masters.*

If we encounter a situation where it seems the government is infringing on these rights, I think the individual will have to resolve between himself, his Christ Self and I AM presence what course to take. There must always be the recourse to the Brotherhood. One must depend on the inner self for direction. At the time I was challenging the Religious Affairs Committee, I did not feel any doubt in my mind and I did not have any fear whatsoever. Because within me I had resolved that I wasn't going to cooperate with the military regime in their persecution of the churches in Ghana.

This inner boldness and courage comes from the empowerment of the Spirit. And unless I had gone within, to the feet of the Brotherhood, I am not sure I would have had the courage to do it.

For more than twenty years, the church in Ghana faced difficult times. During this period I found out that when you stand up to face the tyrants, they back off. The ones who were bold enough to face the military regime were not harmed.

I also realized that in time of difficulties, the people, whether Christians or not, look to the church for leadership. They look to the church as spokesman with the authorities and as intercessor with God.

In order to fulfill this mission, the church must recognize

---

* Jesus' Christmas Day Address 1993, "Render Unto Caesar the Things That Are Caesar's and unto God the Things That Are God's," published in *Pearls of Wisdom,* vol. 36, no. 72.

the nature of the challenge and determine to face it with courage. It must make intense calls on the situation, using specific inserts written covering all areas of concern. The church can also make a detailed written report to the Karmic Board,* bringing to their attention all wrongs and injustices and asking for their adjudication and intercession.

The church must give assurance to members that the Brotherhood will ultimately win, all the while encouraging them to do the spiritual work that will allow the masters to enter in and bring about this victory. The church must provide information on the situation to members and also provide spiritual guidance and counseling where this is needed.

Stay focused and attuned. Do not be distracted by attempts of well-meaning people to put you in contact with "influential" persons in government who can step in and assist you. These people may have their own biases and agendas. Trust not in the arm of flesh. The masters must be your consultants, advocates and guardians. In difficult times, it is necessary to trust the masters absolutely.

---

* The Karmic Board is the council of ascended masters who adjudicate karma, justice and mercy for this system of worlds.

Chapter 32

"Take It to the Lord in Prayer"

Questions of conscience come up in many different ways when one is following the spiritual path. It is often a challenge to know what is the right way to go—when to take a stand on principle, when to try to find some means to avoid an unneeded confrontation.

Issues of principle are often most difficult when they occur within the church itself. From time to time, given human nature, in any organization you will find that people make wrong decisions. Sometimes they get a little power drunk—and then there must be an effective way of checking them. This is why there are checks and balances in the founding documents of most organizations.

If things are heading in a wrong direction, your loyalty, your commitment to the masters, to the Guru, will not allow you to follow. But you don't just rise up one day and say, "I disobey." We are in the church and we desire to be loyal to our church, its leaders, articles, bylaws, the mission and the messengers.

As human beings the tendency may be to say, "If you don't agree with us, then leave the fold." We may feel like doing this at times, and there may be times when to withdraw is the best path. But the burden that is placed on you is that you have to remain true to your conscience.

The teacher who will never leave you is your conscience. If you leave when you could stay and do something to help, or if you compromise your honor, your integrity, by staying and being quiet, it is at the risk of daily being accused by your conscience. And your conscience will never stop accusing you until the day you die, or until you are free from the weight of a wrong decision—when you have made your call for forgiveness and transmutation, made your peace with your God, and you see that the karma has been balanced.

To make the burden easy, you have to take it to the Lord in prayer. There is a song in the Methodist Church which says, "O what needless pain we bear, all because we do not carry everything to God in prayer." And when you are faced with such a situation, you really have to take it to your altar. I think the best way is to write a petition to the masters and set yourself a number of days for a novena. Each day you read the petition and give your novena. At the end of the novena, you burn the petition, and the masters act very swiftly. They really do.

If there is a problem in the church, one thing you must resolve is that it does not go out of the circle of the church, that it does not get into the public domain. That is what one must promise oneself. It is an internal issue. Because there are other forces and individuals outside who would like to blow things out of proportion, to use anything they can to interfere with the work of the masters.

After taking the issue to the altar, the second step is to look within the organization and determine who is the person or what is the body in whose area of responsibility the problem lies. Take the issue to them. Find ways and means of pointing out error, letting people know that a step is a wrong step. And sometimes if you don't act swiftly, you may wake up one day to see that things have reached a point where the situation becomes very difficult to correct. But remember that one often has to deal with such issues in a very cautious and diplomatic manner.

I would say you engage in dialogue first. This dialogue has two purposes. The first is to let the people who are responsible understand the wrongness of the action or the path they are taking. The second is that on the inner, this serves as a reversing of the tide, pushing back the venom behind the wrong action.

Even if you approach this very diplomatically, you may get a negative reaction, even a personal attack. We cannot stop people saying what they want to say about us or from doing what they want to do. But we can always defeat them, and the way to do so is to remember to go to our altar.

Whenever you find a problem, the altar is the place where you have the strongest weapon to deal with it. And always be specific. If a wrong decision has been made or if things seem to be going in a wrong direction, name the names of all the people involved at the altar. That is always where the victory lies.

As you continue to do your spiritual work on the issue, be grateful for the pieces of information that come your way. Do not get scared. No matter what you hear or how bad things may seem, receive the information that comes to you as the opportunity to send your perfect submission to the Brotherhood at the altar.

Chapter 33

An Extension of My Years

My first visit to the church headquarters in America was 1978. The next time was 1981, when Mother invited me to attend Summit University Level II. By 1991, I felt I had been away for a long time and I needed to come back. I have always felt that spiritually the Inner Retreat is our home, and you can't be away from home for ten years. I needed to come back and see what was there, like a refresher. So I wrote to Mother to let her know that I planned to come and that I was thinking of pursuing Summit University Level III.

I had been director of the church in Ghana and all of Africa since January 1982, and I also felt that I needed to step aside and allow someone else to get in the saddle and move on with the mission. So when I arrived at the Inner Retreat, I went to the Office of Ministry to speak with Annice Booth, who was then the director. I said, "Annice, I'm thinking of stepping aside."

She said, "What? Are you 144 years old?"

I said, "No. I am fifty-nine."

And she said, "You are supposed to spend twelve years on each line of the clock. And if you haven't got near that, then don't think of retiring. I am twelve years older than you are, but I'm still working, I'm not thinking of retiring." So we both laughed.

That stuck in my head. Twelve years on each line of the clock would really be something. But if that is so obvious, why did God say threescore years and ten in the Bible? And I kept pondering this in my heart. I concluded that with diligence, and by God's grace, and only by his grace, our years can be extended beyond threescore and ten.

When Mother was blessing me as a lay minister and she made the call to Hilarion to increase my number of years, I was very happy. Since that time I feel that the masters have been protecting me, and it has been my prayer, particularly to Mother Mary, that my years might be extended. And whenever I give this prayer, I always say, "But let those years be filled with strength, determination and commitment to do the masters' work."

Chapter 34

Truth on the Airwaves

In the year 2000, after doing much outreach with public lectures, we felt we needed to reach a wider audience. We had seen the success of our television shows in the 1980s, and we decided that we should try to get on the radio. We made the decision at a meeting of the Ghana Church Board.

Earlier I had gone with Rev. Donkoh to visit a few stations, but we did not get a good response from any of them. So I sent one of our volunteer staff to go around to talk with the radio stations, to see which of them would take us.

He found one station that responded favorably, Channel R, and he came back to tell us that we should meet with them and try to strike a bargain. So I went to meet the commercial manager of the radio station. We sat down and we talked. He said he did not want anything that would be controversial. I said, "Don't worry, the word of God cannot be controversial. Others may have controversial subjects, but not this Church Universal and Triumphant."

So we struck a deal. He quoted a fee, and we signed an agreement for six months. We sent a check and paid for the whole series, twenty-six shows.

The radio show was live every Sunday morning at six o'clock for thirty minutes. The show was called *Keys to the Kingdom*. I would speak for twenty to twenty-five minutes and

167

the rest of the time was phone-ins. It was really wonderful. People would call in with all manner of questions concerning the masters' teachings, what they had heard, and what they had probably read somewhere else. And we answered all of them.

Things were going very well until I preached one week about karma and reincarnation, the missing link in Christianity. I shared Mother's teachings on this subject. I explained that Jesus himself taught reincarnation, and it's right there in the Bible. In Matthew, chapter 11, Jesus says that John the Baptist is Elijah come again. And I said that the pastors and ministers were not telling the truth and that the people wanted their pastors to tell them these things.

This particular show created quite a problem between one of the ministers in another church and his congregation. I understand that one person in that congregation asked that minister, "I heard this and this and that on the radio show by Rev. Kyei. Is it true, all that he said?"

The minister said, "Yes."

This man shot back, "Then why have you not told us?"

That sparked a great deal of controversy in that church. It seems that the Christian Council also felt threatened, so they used their connections with the owner of Channel R to get him to abrogate our agreement. It was a unilateral decision. He did not tell me about it until I showed up to do my program one Sunday morning and I was told, "Sorry, you cannot broadcast anymore."

I said, "What? We have paid for all the shows. We do not owe you. The station still owes us. Who made this decision?"

"The director."

And I said, "He did not even have the courtesy to give me prior notice. You have my phone numbers. You could have at least called to let me know."

Once controversy arose on that issue, I withdrew. When

Mother visited Ghana in 1978, the Christian Council was stirring up opposition. And now, many years later, when they realized that it was Elizabeth Clare Prophet's message that I was giving on the radio, they rose up against it again.

Channel R never did refund our money, and we did not pursue it. The attitude of the station director was so repulsive that I really did not even want to sit down and engage with him.

So we went out looking for another station, and we found Choice FM. We had a lengthy interview with the commercial manager, and he became really enthusiastic. He thought we could have a good message for the people.

In fact, the station went even further. They invited me to appear on a radio program produced by the station itself. I said, half joking, "Well, when I appear on your station with my radio program, you charge me. So if you want me to appear in your program, I should charge you."

They said, "No, no, no. We are promoting your show!"

So while I was doing my own radio program, I also appeared on their show, a discussion program on religious issues. I was on that station for more than six months, once a week. We were on the discussion program for free, but we were paying 600,000 Ghana cedis for each program of our own show. This was a lot of money for us—more than $6,000 for the whole series—but we saw the response of the people in the phone-ins and the enthusiasm for the teachings, and we thought it was worth the expense.

After we had done our radio show for a number of years, we thought we should try to get on television. So in 2005, we did six months on Metro TV and another six months on TV3. It was the same time slot, six o'clock Sunday morning for half an hour, and this show was also called *Keys to the Kingdom*. And oh, the phone-ins. The people who tuned in were really interested in what we had to say.

Even after we had stopped the program, I would meet people on the street who recognized me from the show. They would ask, "What happened to you?"

I said, "We are still here."

"What about your television show?"

"We will be coming again."

"Is it because of money that you stopped?"

"Partially."

"Then make an appeal. We will contribute."

But it wasn't only because of the money that we stopped. It was hard work and time consuming. You have to research, you have to make sure that what you tell the congregation is correct. Every week for a year was quite something. But overall it made a great impression on the people. That was the time when if you mentioned Church Universal and Triumphant, people would say, "Oh, Rev. Kyei's church." That's how we came to be known. I was a media personality for a little while.

We reached most of Ghana with this television show. The staff at TV3 said that their audience was about eight million people. Imagine! In thirty minutes, you reach eight million people with the masters' teachings.

One time I was visiting Nigeria, far away from Ghana, and my phone rang. I picked it up and there was the voice of a man who asked, "Is that Rev. Kyei?"

I said, "Yes."

He said, "Good morning, sir. I have been following your program." He introduced himself and said my television program was one that he never missed. He thought that everything I said on that program was the truth, even though he was a Muslim. And as far as he was concerned, there were only three ministers in Ghana who were worth listening to, and Rev. Kyei was one of them.

I said, "Praise God and thank him, because the message is

the truth."

The masters do indeed have the keys to life. Because in the masters' teachings, there is no controversy, there is no doubt. There is no difference between the truth that the church should preach and what is true in people's own hearts.

The comment I have heard from many people is that in this church, you listen to the masters' words and you immediately feel in your own heart that it is the truth.

Chapter 35

Fifty-Seven Years

While we had our show on TV3, the station also asked me to be on a social program that came on late in the night. On this show we talked about family problems, particularly about marriage. I often spoke about the proper way to go about courtship, the dowry and other things.

On one show I said that if you are going to go into marriage, you have to make up your mind that you are going into a lifelong relationship. It is not a question of going into it as a trial, as some people seem to do these days, to see if you like it—if it doesn't suit me, I quit. I said, "We don't do that. I have been married to my wife for fifty years," which it had been at that time.

The hostess of the program said, "What did you say?"

I said, "My wife and I have been married for fifty years."

She said, "Cheee!"

I said, "What's wrong with that? That is how it should be. She is my partner for life."

She said, "Fifty years! Cheee!" She could not get over it. This was a television program and she had forgotten herself. She was less than thirty years of age.

I said, "Marriage is a lifelong partnership. That's why you need to take your time and find the one who is right for you. You determine that you agree together that you are sharing your life. It is a friendship. If you want a real friend in this world, a reliable friend, apart from God, it is your wife or your husband. If you have any other friends that take precedence over that relationship, the marriage will not work. Jealousy will set in, you will have unnecessary backbiting and gossip."

My wife, Elizabeth, is my partner. When I was in the business field, I would come home and if I had problems with the business I would sit quietly, and she would notice. And she would wait. After I had my meal, I would sit down and want to watch the TV news. She would come and sit by me and say, "Uncle, when you went to work, what happened?"

I would say, "Nothing happened."

And she would say, "I think something happened, because you are not your usual self. You are unusually quiet. Would you like to share with me what it is?"

She would keep asking me until I told her what had happened. Then she would say, "This is no problem. Do it this way, do it that way, do it this way."

I thank God that I married this woman. I applied the suggestions that she gave, and I had my peace and my freedom. Her solutions worked. She has been truly a friend.

Sometimes she would say, "You forget what your mother told me."

"What did my mother say?"

"When your mother was leaving Nsawam, at the railway station she said that I should take you as my father, my uncle, my brother, my everything." And that had sunk deep into her. So even though we live as man and wife, she doesn't think of us as man and wife—she thinks of me as her brother.

She has been a good partner, and we have been married now for fifty-seven years. We have never quarreled—not once. It is very common in our culture to find women always complaining to their mothers-in-law, their fathers-in-law, their relatives, their friends, about their husbands. But Elizabeth doesn't do this. If there is something she does not like, she tells me about it. We have learned that whatever is worrying you, you talk it over and deal with it. Don't harbor it.

Elizabeth is a good woman. She never carried her marriage problems to friends. She would say to them, "You think I am a fool? What marriage doesn't have problems? You have your own problems. And you want me to come and tell you about mine?" This is what she would tell her friends.

So looking back I am very grateful to God that I married this woman.

Chapter 36

"It's Up to You"

I once heard an interesting story from a Catholic priest about the power of prayer.

There was an elderly Catholic lady in Kumasi who was much respected in the community. All the young girls and women in that area trusted her, and they would give her their jewelry to keep. The most precious thing for women in Africa is their jewelry, and these girls knew that wherever they might go, when they would return, this lady would be there and their jewelry would be safe.

Every morning at five o'clock, this lady would walk more than two miles to the Catholic cathedral in Kumasi to attend Mass. One day she got up, went to the cathedral and returned. Whenever she would leave or enter her house, the first thing she would do was to look where the jewelry was. This day when she returned, the jewelry was not there.

She did not make any noise. She did not ask anybody in the house what had happened. She just turned around and walked all the way back to the cathedral. She went and knelt before the statue of Mother Mary, and she said, "Mother, when I came home this morning from Mass, the jewelry from the young ladies in the area that I have been keeping was gone. It wasn't there. You know this jewelry is not mine. It is for these young girls. So how the jewelry is going to come back, whether the jewelry will be back or not be back, it is up to you."

When the Catholic father told me this story, at this point I smiled. It was such a simple prayer. He said, "Elder, don't laugh. That is the simplest prayer that you can offer."

After the old lady said her prayer, she got up and went back home. These days the charismatic people would say that what happened next is a miracle.

When she was about to enter her house, she saw a young man carrying something on his head. He came to her and said, "Old lady, when you went out this morning I came for this, but now I am bringing it back." It was the bundle of jewelry. He had been watching her very carefully for some time, and this morning he had taken it.

She looked at him and said, "Go and put it back where you found it." This man then went in the house, put the jewelry back, and went away.

The lady went straight from her house to the Catholic mission house and told the father what had happened. I was meeting with him later that same day, and we were talking about the efficacy of the rosary. He said, "It is true, the rosary is very powerful," and he told me this story. It is so true. Sometimes prayer acts very, very swiftly, and that baffles the mind.

I smiled. And he said, "Why are you smiling?"

I said, "You are a Catholic priest. But I tell you, I know this even better than you do. Mother Mary acts, and acts very swiftly. If you trust her, she is really a mother. But you have to tell her. She sees it, she knows it. But she's waiting for the specific prayer. If you don't tell her, nothing happens."

I do not know what happened to the man who stole the jewelry, but something did happen because the old lady tossed it over to the Divine Mother. She said, "It's up to you"—in Ashanti, "Eto gye woara." It puts the whole challenge on the

Divine Mother.

When she gave this prayer, I think immediately the energy of malintent returned to the man who stole the jewelry—he was still carrying the bundle, he hadn't even put it down. Injustice cannot stand: God has already pronounced judgment on it. You only have to invoke it. Invoke the judgment, let it fall.

Chapter 37

Healing

When I visited Nigeria several years ago, there was a person in the congregation whose wife was the police commissioner. I asked this Keeper of the Flame where his wife was, and he told me that she was at the hospital. I asked if we could visit her, and he agreed. So we went.

Here was this woman who was the police commissioner, and the doctors had more or less told her it was not going to be possible for her ever to be able to walk again. So we sat down and had a chat. We chatted for quite a while. I asked her how she became sick.

She had been working in a high position as police commissioner, and as a woman having risen to that level, it was clear that she had become the enemy of forces that wanted to commit crime. And from the circumstances she narrated to me about her illness, and from my knowledge of Africa and how prevalent this practice is, I realized that she was the victim of black magic.

Sometimes my Holy Christ Self tells me to ask a question, and in those situations I ask straightforward and awkward questions. So I said, "Commissioner, do you want to go back home to take care of your husband and children?"

I think she did not expect that question, and she was just looking at me. She just lay on the bed and she did not answer.

Her husband felt very uncomfortable, and he started shouting at her, "Did you hear what the minister said? Why don't you answer him?" So I repeated the question about two more times.

She looked at me and said, "This is what the doctors have said: It is impossible for me to be able to walk again. But if I can go home, fine! I would like it. It's okay."

We chatted for a while longer, and then I said, "Let's pray."

And we prayed. I believe it was one of what I call my "unusual prayers," when my voice gets deep, I can have tears in my eyes and I feel within me that my prayer is reaching its target, that what I intend the prayer to do has been accepted. I was thinking she was a victim of black magic, so I asked Archangel Michael to help her and I asked the Elohim Astrea to help. Particularly if I am dealing with issues of witchcraft and black magic, I always call to the Elohim. I always say to myself that it takes the Elohim to dislodge these fallen ones. I will often include a call to the Elohim Cyclopea to give me the vision to see what is the cause and the source of the problem. Of course, I go to Mary and Kuan Yin to intercede and to let the violet flame wash away the sin, the cause and core of any karma that may be involved.

The prayer ended after two or three minutes. Then this woman sat up and started looking under the bed.

The husband said to her, "What are you looking for?"

"My slippers."

"Your slippers? What do want them for?"

"I need my slippers."

The husband found the slippers and gave them to her.

After a while I said, "I would like to say goodbye, because tomorrow I am returning to Ghana."

The woman said, "Let me see you off at the gate."

I had a surprised look on my face, because this is a person who had been in bed for at least two months and the doctors had said it wasn't possible for her to walk again. To see me off at the gate?

She got up, put on her slippers and walked, not briskly, but following us all the way from the ward to the gate of the hospital, which was quite some distance.

The husband could not express his surprise. For two months he had been back and forth to visit his wife, coming and going, looking after his children at home by himself. He had become the mother for his children as well as the father. And here she was walking.

The following day I flew back to Ghana. A week later I called him to find out how his wife was doing. He said, "My wife is with me in the house!"

I said, "What?!"

He said, "Reverend, the day after you left, she was discharged from the hospital." A real miracle. It was one of those things.

I don't know that it is peculiar to me. When someone comes to me for counseling or when I am talking with them, I try to tune in. I place myself in the person's place to get a feel for the origin of their problem. I sit quietly and watch the person and let him or her talk. I listen with all of my being. By the time they have finished speaking, I get the picture.

I remember one lady who came to me. We talked, and then I asked her a very blunt question. I said, "I am going to ask you this, but forgive me and don't be angry with me. Have you ever caused an abortion?"

I did not know her husband or any of her relatives. But as she spoke with me I was prompted to ask that question because she seemed to be somehow harboring a sense of guilt, and she wasn't speaking about it.

She looked down. She was quite shocked. I looked at her reaction and I said, "I am sorry. Forgive me. Don't be surprised.

But I think that is the problem. You have that sense of being guilty about something. This is the reason I felt I should ask you.

"Do you know that this can cause you to not have children in this life? But you are young and you have not reached a stage where you cannot bring forth children. So I would advise you to take some time, talk to your God, and ask to be forgiven for this abortion. Ask your God to forgive you. Tell God that this time you have the willingness to be a mother to life. God will forgive you."

She got up and we parted. I saw that she was relieved and happy. I have not found out if she did receive another child or not. But at least she was relieved of a burden.

If you are a minister, many people may come to talk with you about issues that are burdening them. I have learned that if you have patience and allow the person to talk with all of their heart, you will get the answer to the problem from what they say.

I often ask them to write a letter asking for forgiveness. I remember Mother said that in our approach to the Godhead, the first step in any situation is to call upon the law of forgiveness. I have never forgotten that.

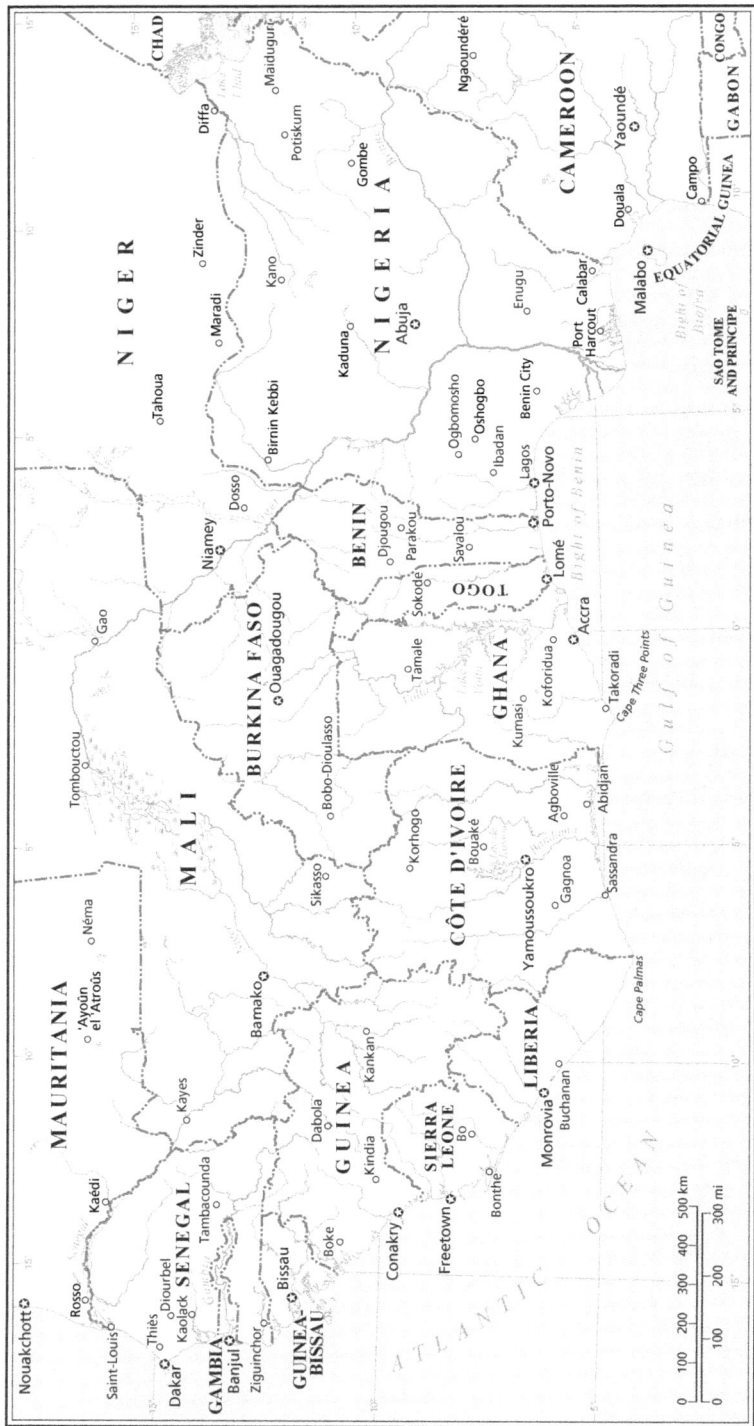

Chapter 38

Missionary Work

Being a missionary in Africa is not easy. In many places, safety is a real concern. For example, in eastern Nigeria, it is not safe to travel by road. They have rebels—some call them terrorists—fighting the government over oil money. They kidnap people for ransom. The only safe way to travel is to fly from city to city.

In December 2010 I was in Calabar, in the east of Nigeria, and they wanted me to go to another center. I have been there several times in earlier years, but now it is not safe. I told the leader from the other group, "I am sorry, I cannot go. The road network isn't good, the roads are very rough. Secondly, there are these kidnappings going on. I am not from that area. If they happen to kidnap me, who is going to pay the ransom for my freedom?" It is very unsafe for a white person. It is even unsafe for Africans.

On a previous visit to Nigeria, I flew into Lagos, the capital, and spent some time there. After that, I flew to the eastern part of the country and visited four states to do outreach: Rivers State, Cross-River State, Akwa Ibon State and Abia State. Arrangements had already been made to hire the halls where we would hold lectures and meet the public.

I flew to Nigeria alone on that occasion, but I always travel with someone when I reach the country. So when I left Lagos to go to the east, Edna and Joseph, two Nigerian Keepers of the Flame, came with me. I flew, but they went by road and met me when I arrived there.

They put me in a hotel. We all sat down, we talked, we discussed issues. Then Joseph and Edna left for where they were going to stay, and they left me alone at this hotel. I think this was my third visit to this place, so I was not expecting anything unusual to happen.

However, some time later, I was in my room when the reception rang and told me that I had a visitor. They did not wait to ask me whether I wanted to see him or not. Then I heard a knock on the door. I opened the door and there was a big man standing there. He said, "Are you Rev. Kyei, the man from Ghana?"

I said, "Yes."

"Reverend, can I come in?"

"Please come in."

I did not know that man from Adam, and it wasn't right for me to do this, it wasn't safe for me to invite him into my room, but I did not expect anything strange to come of it. I thought he was interested in the teachings and had seen our poster outside. So I brought him in.

He started asking me why I was there, where I came from. Then he said, "Do you have some coke?"

And I said, "Maybe you can ask the reception, they may sell it."

"No, I am not asking about Coca-Cola drink. I mean coke."

I said, "What coke?"

I thought he meant Coca-Cola, but he was talking about cocaine. When I said this, he realized that I was so green, I didn't know what he was talking about.

Then he changed his line of approach. He started talking

about what I was there for and what was the nature of our teaching and other general things.

I had a small camera and he asked if he could take photographs, because he thought maybe there was cocaine hidden in the camera. So I snapped a few photos for him.

After that he said, "Sir, I come from the SSS (the State Security Service). We had information that a visitor had come here, and because of the nature of the information that was given, I was sent to take you from the hotel to the SSS station."

When he came and saw me, he realized that this was not the kind of person to deal in this type of thing. So he decided to sit down and talk, and after asking all those questions, he realized that this wasn't my line.

Before he left, he said, "Watch these people at the reception at the hotel. They sent me here."

That was a very unpleasant experience. The Nigerian SSS is known to be very rough. The people in Nigeria know that most of these state security men are not civil at all. If this man had even a little suspicion, he would have taken me to the station to be interrogated. But the masters protected me.

I didn't say anything to the people in the hotel. I waited until Edna came from where she was staying. I told her what had happened. I said to her, "Why did you put me here? If you knew the security wasn't normal in this area, why did you leave me alone in this hotel? If that man had been rough and had gone strictly according to his instructions, he could have taken me to the station. None of you who are my close friends would have even known where I was. If it was the hotel that gave the information, they would likely say, 'Oh, he has gone out.' They would not care." I was a bit cross with Edna.

She went to see the hotel manager and his staff and she really let them have it. She was so furious. She gave them some very heated words. We left the hotel immediately and I checked in to a different one. In fact, I was so upset about what had happened that if it had not been my determination to continue with what I was meant to do, I would have cancelled the outreach meeting. But we held the outreach as planned and did not tell the other members of the group there what had happened until we were about to leave.

This is the kind of difficult situation we sometimes meet when we go out in Africa, because in many countries we do have, for want of better words, bad leaders—people in power who do not want others to share that power. They treat their people very badly. They become tyrants, then they have security police, who also behave in a very rough manner to their own people. It is a problem in many countries.

Cameroon is the next country to the east of Nigeria. There was a Keeper of the Flame there with whom I had been corresponding over the years. One time I asked him to arrange for a visit so we could hold a public lecture and officially inaugurate the group there. They had about six or eight people who met regularly to give decrees.

We were about to fix a date for me to fly to the country, when I asked him if he was sure it was okay for me to come. He said, "Oh, Reverend, I think we have to wait for a while."

I said, "Why?"

The problem was that the group could not meet in one location more than once. They had to meet here this week and a different place the following week. If you would meet in the same place, the third time you would have the secret police calling on you. So they had to keep moving their meetings from one place to another.

I said, "I won't risk it. I have more to do than to risk this kind of situation in one country."

So we called it off. I don't know whether he is still there or if he has been transferred or what happened to him. I never heard from him again.

I have been to South Africa and Kenya, and I have not had any problems in these countries. I was invited to the Democratic Republic of the Congo* once, but it was in the area where they had the civil war so it was not safe to go there.

My experience has been that the French speaking nations are often the ones where the people have less freedom in their political systems. Even just across the border from Ghana, in Togo, it is not safe to have a group. If you are not Catholic or one of the orthodox churches, you will have the police coming to find out what you are doing. They become suspicious. And if they find out that the organization has its roots in America, it is even more of a problem. In some African nations the word CIA has become a frightening thing, and they think that any connection with America is indicative of involvement with the CIA.

Sometimes the current problems in these nations have their roots in how they were founded. There is violence because the foundation was violent. The first leader of Congo-Kinshasa was Patrice Lumumba, who was trained in a freedom-fighters' school in Ghana.

Kwame Nkrumah, the first president of Ghana, set up this training camp. When they sent people there, they put them in a plane and flew around and around so they thought that they were flying a long way, out of Ghana. Then they would land at night and take them out to that camp. It was quite close to my village, an old mining site about two miles away by bush road. It was fenced so no one could get in.

Patrice Lumumba was trained there, and he went to the Congo to agitate for freedom from the Belgians. The Belgians

---

* The Democratic Republic of the Congo was formerly known as Zaire, and before that the Belgian Congo. This nation is also commonly known as Congo-Kinshasa, Kinshasa being its capital city. The neighboring Republic of the Congo, formerly a French colony, is known as Congo-Brazzaville.

had their own stooges and also plotted against Lumumba. It was a violent thing, they tortured him. He had his supporters, and there was a civil war.

The nation was founded on violence, and they have never known peace since they became independent in 1960. This nation is at the level of the solar-plexus chakra of the African continent. The solar-plexus chakra is the chakra of the sixth ray, the ray of peace, and this is what should be there. Instead, there is agitation and war. The United Nations report on the civil war showed that many of the women have been violated by the rebels and even the government troops. They murdered some Ghanaian troops who were there as part of a peace-keeping mission.

The Congo is following the same path as Somalia, but on a different scale. It is a very vast country, enormously wealthy in natural resources. If the lightbearers there can rise up and put down the forces of darkness that have oppressed them, if they can clear the records of the past with the violet flame, their nation can be a great force for the light on the continent of Africa.

Chapter 39

Our Brother Afra

To someone who has never heard of the Ascended Master Afra, this is what I would say:

We know that individuals are often named after some great man, who can even be a family member, an uncle, a grandfather. So are nations. And so Africa is a big continent that is named after a great, great soul who lived a life of virtue and love and compassion, a life of brotherliness.

This great man is called Afra. They say he is called "a *frater*," the Latin word for "brother." This brother lived long ago, and he taught people to love one another and to regard all as brothers and sisters. What he loved to show men was the unity that should exist above all. That is what he set before the people and what he talked about and preached.

He is a great man and his greatness cannot be matched by anyone presently on our continent. He is loving and very handsome. If you should see his face, you would know it is the face of love and compassion. If all of us living on the soil of Africa, and not only Africa but throughout this planetary home, would take up his teaching, peace would be everywhere.

But as has happened to many other great men, some people did not like him and what he taught. And as they plotted against the Lord Jesus Christ, so Afra was plotted against, and they killed him, as they did Jesus. We are told that this event happened over half a million years ago.

Afra became an ascended master, and I can tell you that he is alive and very much involved with the people and the events in Africa today. You may wish to try him by asking him, "Brother Afra, help me to be loving and compassionate as you are." Who knows? Perhaps he will really be your friend.

There is a little village in the Volta region in the eastern side of Ghana. There was a woman trader in that village who was very generous and helpful to the people. She received a male visitor one day who stayed with her for a few days. When the man left, the lady asked for his name. He said, "It doesn't matter." He didn't tell his name. He went away.

The same time the following year, this visitor came again, stayed with them for about a week, and then left. Once more she asked his name, and he said again, "No, it doesn't matter."

There is a mountain by this village, and a waterfall—very beautiful. She thought that maybe he was a man who was looking for waterfalls or places where tourists might visit.

The third year at the same time he returned, stayed with them for another week. This time before he left he asked the woman to take him to the village chief, and she did.

The man told the village chief, "Take care of that woman, because she is a point of unification and she is capable of bringing all the people together." He told the chief that in future that place was going to be a center where all the villages around would come together for the development of the area. The chief thanked him.

The woman took her visitor back home. When the man had said goodbye to her and he was about to leave, she said, "This time you have to tell me your name. What is your name?

He said, "Afra." And he gave her a piece of cloth as a gift. He would not wait for any further discussion. He told his name, gave her the present and off he went. I was given that piece of cloth, and I still have it.

This happened around the year 2000. True to what Afra said, the village is expanding. They have a tourist board which has developed the waterfall to become a tourist attraction, and they are receiving more visitors. The woman happens to be the mother of one of our ministers, and she passed on in 2010.

People sometimes ask me, "Have you seen Afra? Can you describe him?" And I will say, "Yes." It happened in South Africa.

On one of my visits a few years back, I was speaking about Afra to the community. And lo and behold, he appeared—tall, medium build, very, very handsome. And his presence expanded to fill almost the whole room, as if we were all living within him.

I smiled and I said, "Do you see Afra?"

They all looked surprised. I saw him with my inner eye, but no one else saw him.

This beautiful man—when you look at his face, it is so serene, very calm. His love and his great heart can be seen in his face. If you were to see him, I think you would love him at first sight. This is Afra. He looked like the portrait that we have, except that the face was a little broader than the picture.

When I saw him, and again when I heard the story of Afra appearing in the east of our country, my mind went back to the dictation that Afra gave in Ghana in 1976. He said, "I walk the streets of Accra every day. When I see the lack of unity among the people, I rend my garments."

Then I thought of the tragedy of disobedience that led to the fall of man—such a serious tragedy, because all of the beauty and joy that we could have been enjoying all this time was lost to us.

The real and exclusive revelation by the Lord, the Christ Self, the Mighty I AM Presence, the beauty of the beyond,

The Ascended Master Afra

cannot be described in any words here on earth. The serenity and the feeling of joy in the heart of each one in the higher octaves is beyond what we find in the physical. In heaven there is no pretension on the part of any individual. There is no struggle. You don't have to think of the way to go, because the way is natural. In the beyond, joy and beauty are the natural flow of life.

Chapter 40

The Good Shepherd

When you are looking to set up a new group to study the teachings of the masters, I think it begins by way of conversation. When you have a friend or someone you think is interested in the esoteric path, you engage this person in conversation. You have a book that you think will interest him or her and you lend it and let him or her read it for a while.

If it seems there may be some interest, schedule some visits with the person, ask a few questions concerning the book and what he has read. You always watch to see the level of interest. If he doesn't express any interest, don't press it. If you push, you will spoil the whole thing. So go about it in a very gingerly manner. If you find out that there is real interest, then you can arrange to invite him or her to see a video.

I suggest they watch something with the messenger so they make eye contact with her. Mother is a beautiful soul, and watching her talking, you cannot fail to be impressed. I would always prefer that those who are seeking have that face-to-face contact. You can have this in your home in quite an informal way. If the setting is too formal they might feel less comfortable. The video shouldn't be long. Half an hour is good. If the video is longer, stop after half an hour so that they leave longing for more.

This is all a testing period. I call this an exploratory stage, trying to find out the person's level of genuine interest in the teachings. Try to encourage questions. If the person doesn't ask questions this may be a sign of less interest, in which case you don't press it further.

However, there are some who don't say much who need to be encouraged, because for some people who are searching, when the masters' teachings are introduced the first time, they may get confused. There is so much depth in the teachings, they may find it even mind-boggling. This is particularly the case these days in Africa, where we have so many charismatics pushing trash into the minds of the people.

Introduce people to the teachings in a very gradual manner. If the person shows real interest, keep it up. Then you can look for another person. When you have two or three, form a little group that meets at a fixed time each week. Show a video for half an hour. Encourage them to talk and ask questions. Even if people have a spiritual background, the masters' teachings are different from what they have come from. So encourage them to talk to let you know what they think. These meetings shouldn't be lengthy. Forty-five minutes to an hour is fine. If it should be prolonged, let the desire come from them.

In forming a new group, always encourage the members to participate actively. The leader doesn't have to cook everything for them. Let them decide. When they are involved, they will be happy. When they know that it's their decision, their own thinking that is setting the direction, they will want to participate.

From this exploratory stage, we encourage them to register as Keepers of the Flame. Give each one the Keepers of the Flame brochure to read after one or two videos or one or two sessions, when you are certain that they have an interest. The length of the exploratory stage depends on the people. There are those who are past a certain stage on the inner, who come in and after two or three sessions ask how they can join. Others need a more lengthy introductory period.

Most people in Ghana attend church on Sunday morning, so Sunday afternoon is a good time in the beginning for regular weekly meetings. People can go to their own churches on Sunday morning and then the Summit meeting in the afternoon. From that stage the rest depends on them. What do they want to do? At some point they might hold outreach events in the local area to bring more people.

You need to have spiritual work, or it won't last. They must also be taught at every meeting. If the meeting is one hour, I will use the first fifteen minutes for spiritual work, learning about decrees and giving them together. I use the next half hour for studies. The book *The Science of the Spoken Word* is good to start with. The last fifteen minutes, I introduce another decree, which would be the first one we would do next week in the opening spiritual work. Each meeting you introduce one more decree, and that's how you gradually build their experience with decrees.

When you introduce a new decree, teach about it first. Then they understand why they're giving the decree. The first decree I teach is the tube of light and violet flame from the "Heart, Head and Hand Decrees." The second decree must be a protection decree to Archangel Michael. "Traveling Protection" is good because everybody needs that and they can give it easily, even when they're going from their homes to their workplaces. Everyone in Africa wants protection because they know there is so much black magic. Next after this are other violet flame decrees, such as "The Law of Forgiveness," "O Saint Germain, Send Violet Flame" and "I AM the Violet Flame."*

When you meet once a week, they should also know that

---

* These decrees and many more may be found in *Prayers, Meditations and Dynamic Decrees for Personal and World Transformation*, published by The Summit Lighthouse. www.TSL.org. "I AM the Violet Flame" may be found on p. 291.

this is still the beginning. You have offered them an introductory program. Let them know what else is available, and let them choose what they would like to do in addition. The healing service on Wednesday evening is very popular, because everyone wants healing. They might like to meet for that once a week, or if that is too much, once a fortnight or once a month. Depending on how the subject is introduced you explain the green ray and the healing flame, what it does, what to expect. It is also the ray of abundance, something everybody loves to have. They will think they can get a magic wand and money will manifest for them!

The decree book covers all of man's needs on planet Earth. Mostly what people are looking for is protection, abundance, and the blood of Jesus, which is the violet flame. They need to be sealed in the tube of light, so they should be introduced to the protection and blue-flame decrees. However, you can sit down and ask for protection and give those decrees twenty-four hours a day, but if the system is polluted and not cleansed it won't be sufficient. They need to know that the violet flame really works, and in Africa they often understand it better when you say it is the blood of Jesus. Unfortunately the charismatics and Pentecostals in Africa have made the blood of Jesus somewhat unappealing, so we need to go beyond that to explain it.

This teaching works wonderfully where the people have someone to teach them. Especially what they need to understand is the background to the decrees. People need education for this teaching to work. For any group to survive, to be firm, to expand, there must be education.

Beginning a study group from scratch, you need to seize the opportunity to talk about the teachings with friends. Some feel too shy to do this, so it is important to learn how to talk with others about the teachings. I think the first step is always to appeal to the Holy Spirit to guide us. If you have the desire to share the teaching with others, talk to the Holy Spirit and say, "Lord, this is my desire, to share the teaching with others. I have the desire, but I don't know how to even go about it. So help me, Lord."

Seek the guidance of the Holy Spirit. Make friends with the Lord, the Maha Chohan, the representative of the Holy Spirit to the Earth, and go about getting the Holy Spirit. And very consciously make yourself the disciple of your own Holy Christ Self. He is the one you have with you always. He is waiting to be asked.

Sometimes we find that even in our sleep we are teaching or being taught. When you have those experiences, even in your sleep, it's important to take note of them and to write them down, because they are going to guide you. You may remember something that is important.

The study group is the basic platform for establishing the teachings, and it is from the study group that you grow to be a teaching center, which is a greater level of commitment and receives a greater level of sponsorship from the masters. At the study group level, it is like the kindergarten or class I. If you have a good teacher who gives the foundation, the lessons are easy for the pupils. But if they miss the foundation, it can be difficult to catch up and they may produce very wrong musical tones. That is why they need to hear Mother.

There are people all over Africa (and all over the world) who could be interested in the teachings, but they need a leader. Sometimes they don't even know that they are looking for someone to be the shepherd. But most people who belong to religious groups want someone to be a leader, to organize, to arrange things. They just want to come and listen and then leave. So in setting up a group in a new area, the first thing that is needed is someone who will be the leader.

We held a two-day outreach recently in Bolgatanga, in the

far north of Ghana. At the end of the second day, as we were closing, one of the new people asked, "Why can't we have a group here? We must have a group." He took it upon himself to form a group and convinced about five of the others to meet with him. There were some other people in the area who had some knowledge about The Summit Lighthouse, and this man offered to contact them, tell them that a center was being set up, and invite them to come.

Such a person has probably passed a certain level of commitment to the path on the inner, and he is ready to move forward. The masters have their disciples all over the world. Many are only waiting for someone to provide the contact that will awaken the inner call.

Chapter 41

Travel in Africa

Early in 2010, I was invited to visit a group of Keepers of the Flame in Congo-Brazzaville. Rev. Emmanuel Asiedu-Mante and my assistant, Nada Donkoh, went with me, and we flew first of all to Lomé, the capital of Togo. From there we flew to Malabo, in Equatorial Guinea, which is where our trouble started.

We got there and we were going through immigration, and one of the officials, I think from the immigration police, took our passports. He didn't tell us anything. We followed him and he ushered us into a big hall where there were a lot of people. He closed the door and it had an electronic lock with a code. Once you get in, you can't get out. Nobody was telling us anything. Another girl came and collected our tickets. Now we had no passports, no tickets.

We managed to find the official who had collected our passports and asked him, "Where are our passports?"

"You don't speak French? I don't speak English."

"But you understood English when you collected our passports. Now we want to know what has happened to our passports." He just pretended that he didn't understand us. So we sat there some more.

Then we went looking for the girl who collected our tickets, but we couldn't find her. Finally they thought we might be hungry, so they took us to a restaurant to eat and then brought us back again. Emmanuel went to ask one of the officers about the passports but he brushed him off.

Then I saw the officer who had collected our passports. We had arrived there at two o'clock and by then it was five or six o'clock. I wanted to ask him what we should do if the place closed. Who could we ask for our passports then? They should at least tell us something.

There were some gentlemen around and I thought one of them looked like he might speak English. So I appealed to him. I asked him to find out what had happened to our passports.

The man asked me, "You don't speak French?"

I said, "No."

He said, "Where are you going?"

"Congo."

"If you don't speak French, why are you going to Congo?" And he walked away. He would not help me. In this part of Africa, they pretend that you don't have any brains.

I told Emmanuel and Nada, "Don't worry. Let's sit down here. At least when night falls we are in a room. They won't throw us outside."

We stayed there until it was about nine or ten o'clock before someone came and asked us, "Are these your passports?"

So they finally gave us our passports.

We asked, "Where is the plane that is supposed to take us to Congo?" He didn't know.

They had turned off all the signs, so we did not know what was happening with the flights. We just had to wait.

Finally, a flight was called. We didn't know where it was going, but I said, "Let's join the line. If it's not our flight they will tell us to leave."

We joined the line and it happened to be for our flight. So we got on board and flew to Congo, to the city of Pointe-Noire.

Instead of 5 p.m., we arrived there at 1 a.m. Fortunately, Barnabe, the leader of the group, was still waiting for us at the airport.

We went through immigration. Here, too, the guy in the cage collected our passports. He did not tell us anything. So we waited. Finally, everyone else from the plane had gone. The official told us, "Come back tomorrow."

We said, "What? Why tomorrow?"

Fortunately, Barnabe was with us in the arrivals hall. He went to ask the official what was happening, and the official said they had given us a paper visa, so he would need to work on it and stamp the passports later, and we should come back the following day. Barnabe assured us that there was nothing wrong.

So we went to collect our baggage. Everyone had collected their baggage, but ours was not there. No baggage. We went to the lost baggage office to complain that our baggage was lost. I saw a man at the desk there, and I said to Emmanuel, "This guy is a security guard, he is a watchman. He won't know about the bags." Emmanuel said, "He is the one at the desk. Let's talk to him."

So we told the man at the desk that our bags were missing. He went over to his computer and he came back. "What type of bags do you have?" He gave us a catalog and we pointed out the bags that looked like ours. He went back to his desk, worked some more on the computer and came back. "What is the color of the bags?"

Emmanuel looked at me, and I said, "Don't look at me. I told you that this man is not the baggage clerk." We told him the color. He went back to his computer and worked a bit more.

He came back and said, "What is the weight?"

Emmanuel said, "Let's go. This man can't tell us anything."

So we were taken to the hotel. Here we were in Congo with

no luggage, with nothing but the clothes that we wore from Accra. And all my lecture notes for the two days were in my bag.

The following day we called the airline office. I said, "Why don't you call Malabo, the place where we stayed for eight hours. Ask them to check if the bags are there." The man at the baggage office said he had sent them three e-mails already, no reply.

We were supposed to fly out that Sunday, after the event finished. On the Friday, I told Barnabe, "Go to the airline office and make sure that our flight is still leaving when it is supposed to."

Barnabe said, "Oh, don't worry. They will do it."

I said, "Hey, don't just tell me they will do it. Go there personally and check." He didn't want to. I said, "Okay. I'll go with you myself." I was concerned about the seminar, but because of the difficulties we had in getting to Congo, I was also concerned about getting home. I wanted to be a step ahead.

So we went to the airline office. They said, "Oh, you are not going on Sunday. The flight has been postponed to Wednesday. We were not able to inform you." In this part of the world, they might wait a few days if they don't have enough passengers for the flight. They fly when they have enough people. They had all our phone numbers there, but they never called us.

The seminar started on Saturday. Fortunately, I have given these lectures many times, so I had most of the thoughts in my head. I was able to give the lectures from memory and from a few notes I was able to write down, and they went well.

There were many people at the public lecture, the hall was full. We had an interpreter. That Sunday we had a service, and the room where we held this meeting was also full. They had to put more chairs outside. After the service there, we held what

I call an "open forum"—an opportunity for people to ask any questions they may have. Many of them were worried about witchcraft and black magic, which is a normal concern for Africans. The people of Africa actually live in fear of these forces all the time. I told them there is a way out of all of this. We have the Science of the Spoken Word.

The seminar concluded on the Sunday. We stayed another three days and left Pointe-Noire on Wednesday. The plane took us to Brazzaville, where we stopped to pick up more passengers, and then to Malabo. We found someone there who spoke English and asked him to find someone we could talk to about our baggage. He said, "Wait here. I will find someone to speak to you."

He brought someone over to us and we explained to this officer the problem of our baggage. The officer disappeared for a couple of hours, and then he came back with Nada's bags and Emmanuel's bags.

I said, "What about mine?"

"Well, your bag didn't come. Maybe you have to check at Lomé."

"Please, can I go with you to the room where the bags are and look for myself?"

So he took me there. They didn't even have a storage room . They just dumped the bags in the office where they were work-ing. I saw my bag. It was very dirty. I said, "That's my bag."

They said, "All right, take it."

That's how we got our bags back. They had been sitting there in Malabo for a week. But our problems were not over yet.

We got on the plane to go home and they told us the plane was not going to Accra.

"Where is the plane flying to?"

"Togo. You will get off the plane at Lomé airport."

We said, "But how do we get to Accra? It is more than a hundred miles away."

They said, "When you reach Togo, we will talk about that."

So we got off the aircraft at Lomé and went to the arrival lounge. Someone came up and asked, "Where is your yellow card?"

"Where is what?"

He said, "Your yellow card."

For the first time on this trip I raised my voice—I feel sorry for the guy—and I said, "Who are you to ask for a yellow card? What do you want a yellow card for? Please, don't disturb us." I was angry, and he went away.

We went to the airline office and we saw an agent and told her our problems. I told Emmanuel that I was fed up with these people and he should negotiate with them. So Emmanuel spoke to her. She finally agreed that they would hire a taxi to take us to Accra.

We got to the taxi and we found out that what the airline had agreed to pay was less than the taxi fare. So Emmanuel agreed to pay the difference. We had arrived in Togo at two o'clock in the afternoon, and it was about five o'clock by the time we had arranged the taxi.

We packed all our things in the taxi. But when we started to drive off a policeman suddenly started shouting at us, banging on the taxi and telling us to stop. Another policeman pulled out his weapon.

The driver stopped. He said, "What's the problem?"

"Where are you going?"

The policeman had been standing beside the car while our bags were being loaded, and he didn't say anything then. He waited until we started to drive off, and then he showed us where the power was. He asked the driver to reverse back.

The driver said, "He is going to detain us. He wants money.

You are elderly people. Go and talk to him."

I told Emmanuel, "I'm not going to be part of this. You go and talk to him."

Emmanuel went and talked with the taxi driver, and the taxi driver negotiated with the policeman about how much money they would need to let us leave. Emmanuel gave the money to the driver and the driver gave it to the policeman. Then he said we could go.

The taxi took us to the Togo-Ghana border. The border is just a line on the road with the Togo immigration office on one side and the Ghana office on the other side. So we got out of the taxi and crossed from the Togo side to the Ghana side. The Ghana immigration officer said, "Do you have your passports?"

"Yes."

"Are you finished with those guys?"

We said, "Yes."

"Please go."

Incidentally, this was the same border that they wouldn't let Mother cross when she was in Ghana and tried to travel by road to Nigeria. She had to return to Ghana because she refused to pay the money that the Togo border officials wanted to let her cross their country.

We hired another taxi and we got back to Accra around eight o'clock. That was really something, quite an experience.

In spite of all the challenges of the journey, the visit to Congo was a great success for the masters and their mission. You could see the people were so interested. They really wanted the teachings. My mind goes back to recall their faces, their joy, their desire for the teaching, how much they wanted to know more. That more than compensated for all the problems we had faced.

Chapter 42

The Need for a Sound Foundation

In earlier years, we had very few members in Kenya. I would occasionally receive correspondence from people there, but it was never enough to encourage me to think seriously about going there. Then one year I came to the July Conference at headquarters and I met a Brazilian man and his wife who were living in Kenya. He told me that he had a group there, about forty people. He had taught them to decree and they were decreeing every day. I said, "It is beautiful to hear what is happening there. We shall see what we can do to help."

When I was back in Ghana, this man wrote to me about the group and asked me to visit. They wanted a formal inauguration of the group. I said, "All right, we will go."

I prepared myself, and Emmanuel, Nada and myself fixed the date. Kenya and Ghana are both British Commonwealth countries, so we didn't need a visa. We jumped on the Kenya Airways plane, a direct flight, six hours from Accra to Nairobi, and the Brazilian man was at the airport waiting for us. It was easy.

There was a Keeper of the Flame in Nairobi who owned a big mansion, her family home. Her husband had left and he was living with another woman. The woman had turned part of the property to a hotel, and that was where we lodged.

We met with the group. First we met for a formal meeting.

There were many people. We talked and we allowed them to ask questions. That was the first day.

On Friday we had the first seminar, and there were quite a number of people. Kenya is a multiracial society, and many of those who came were Pakistanis and Indians. They were a mixture of Hindus, Muslims and Christians. I would say that these were the "liberal" Muslims.

It was very interesting to see the reaction when we would talk of karma, because they do not expect a church with a Christian background to speak about karma. That intrigued them. And they were very happy and very interested.

I think the political issues of the country may have been a factor in so many Indians and Pakistanis being interested in the teachings. They are a small percentage of the population, and there is mistrust between them and the Africans, who are mostly mainline Christians.

Part of the problem is that the Asians had collaborated with the British against the Africans in Kenya at the time of the Mau Mau Uprising, a terrible and bloody period of Kenya's history. So the Africans did not have a liking for the Asians, and when the tables were turned and the political power shifted, a lot of the businesses owned by the Asian community were taken over. In the neighboring country, Uganda, that crazy man Idi Amin confiscated Asian-owned businesses and forced many of them to leave the country. Some stayed but there were lingering fears and mistrust on both sides.

So when the Asians in Kenya found us, a Christian church, coming to talk about karma and reincarnation, they thought this might be different. They were not afraid. They thought they would not find the kind of animosity they might find in a regular African church.

We had our second seminar on the Saturday. Our event lasted two days, and people stayed the whole time. There were about a dozen of them, and if I had been able to continue with them, there could have been more.

There was one minister who came to the event. He had his own church and he had travelled four hundred miles by road to Nairobi for our seminar. It took him about two days. He was very, very happy. He said, "This is the teaching for me."

He said that he would like to see the teaching given to people in his own area. We talked about this, and we agreed that on my next visit to Kenya, I should visit his area. He has formed a group of churches there, kind of a council, and he was going to tell them about us. We would fix the date and would make it like a crusade. All of the churches would meet and I would address them.

On Sunday we met in the sanctuary that was used by the group. We formally inaugurated the group and appointed officers and a board of trustees. They had rented a place where they met. It was quite expensive, but it was in a good area. We had a nice service, but there was a challenge. Right in the middle of the service, the electricity went out. We made calls and decrees until the power came on again. We continued to the finish, and then we baptized children and adults.

It was a good day. The people had good prospects. But we found out that the leader did not start the group on a good footing. He used to help people come to the group by providing them with money for transport. Otherwise they would not be able to afford the fares to get from their homes to the center and back. I told the leader that he had done well, but that this did not lay a sound foundation for the group.

About a week after we consecrated the center, the Brazilian man was transferred to Israel. From Israel he wrote to me about the religious discrimination he found there. They don't want Jews to leave the Jewish faith or join other faiths.

The situation in Africa is similar. Sometimes the family

pressures in the local environment do not make it easy for people to accept another path apart from their traditional faith. Indians in India did not take up the teachings when they were presented there. Indians in Kenya are far away from home, so they are more free to pursue a different path.

After the Brazilian man left Kenya, the group there had great difficulties. There was no more money for transport, and only a few of them could afford to attend services. There were also problems with disunity. The secretary of the group wrote to tell me that the new president was not being helpful and cooperative, so she was resigning.

They had difficulty finding a meeting place. The former leader of the group had been paying the rent where they were, and without him they could not afford it. He asked them to find another place and said he was willing to give them a hundred dollars a month for the rent, but they could not get a place for that price in the center of the city, where it would be easy for people to come. The lady who turned part of her property to a hotel was in a wealthy area, far away from where the members lived. People did not have the means to get there, so they couldn't meet there.

There were about forty people in the group when we visited, and it gradually dwindled until there are now about four, meeting in someone's house. The current leader wrote asking me to visit again. I said, "Fine, no problem. But you don't have a meeting place. Where will you meet with the people?" I have not heard back from her, but I am keeping the communication lines open. I will find out what concrete plans she really has.

It is a challenge to establish a new center and to sustain it. Centers can ebb and flow, but shepherds are needed for the sheep.

Chapter 43

The Holy Spirit

Sierra Leone is a small country in West Africa which was devastated by a civil war in the 1990s. Tens of thousands were killed and many more were mutilated in atrocities committed both by the rebels and the government forces.

There was a gentleman in Sierra Leone called Alfred who was trying to help the thousands of people still living in refugee camps years after the war ended. He found on the Internet a woman who ran an orphanage in South Africa, and he began corresponding with her. A lot of people had died, a lot of children in the camps did not have their parents, and he thought if he could set up a similar organization in his country, that would help.

So he invited this woman to Sierra Leone to help him. She happened to be a member of our church, and when she was there she taught him and his friends about our teachings and taught them to decree. They saw the value of the teachings and the difference it could make. So along with the other work they were doing, Alfred and his friends decided that they should also set up an official Summit Lighthouse study group in their country.

They asked the woman from South Africa to come to Sierra Leone to help them do this, but she knew that this was beyond her. So she referred Alfred to Emmanuel, the leader of the

Ghana group. Emmanuel felt that he could not do it, so he approached me. I said, "It is another opening, another field of service, so we will go." This was in 2009. We arranged to travel to Sierra Leone to do some outreach and formally inaugurate a study group there.

I did not know the difficulties that lay ahead. I thought that the whole event was to take place in Freetown, the capital of Sierra Leone. I was mistaken. Emmanuel and I flew to Freetown, and then we had to make the rest of the journey by road. It was more than two hundred miles and a pretty bad road to Koidu City, in the east of the country. It took six hours to get there. We arrived in the dead of night. Emmanuel was talking about the difficulties of our journey, so I said, "This is the joy of the missionary. If it were not for the love of the people you are serving, you would not do it."

Alfred took us to three different refugee camps for those who had suffered in the war. Many of the people had had limbs amputated—one leg cut off, one hand. You couldn't imagine that human beings would be so cruel to one another. We did not lecture at these camps, we just visited. I did not have the heart to observe all of the pain.*

Alfred and some others had formed the nucleus of a group. They had hired a hall and arranged for us to give a public lecture on Friday and another on Saturday. Alfred is a good organizer. He knew the needs of the people, so he bought rice and prepared a meal for everyone. The people who came to the event knew that after sitting and listening to a lecture about the teachings for two or three hours, they would get something to eat. Getting food can be quite a problem for those who live in the camps.

The hall they had hired was very big, but it could not hold

---

* The movie *Blood Diamond* (2006), starring Leonardo DiCaprio, graphically portrayed the atrocities that occurred in Sierra Leone during the civil war.

all the people who came, and many were standing outside. There were a thousand people there and a thousand again on Saturday. Alfred was surprised, but not completely surprised. He had thought with the inducement of food, there would be a lot. How do you feed a thousand people? How many bags of rice does it take?

I was surprised to see so many. I have never come across that large a crowd in any of my outreach lectures. I had my charts from Djwal Kul's book on the aura, and then I spoke about karma and reincarnation, which I think was an ideal subject for them.

For them to understand, you have to speak the way that they speak, simply. If you speak as if you are addressing university graduates or undergraduates, you miss the boat. Most of them do not speak English. They speak Krio, a mixture of English and native languages. Alfred's brother had become an interpreter, so I spoke and he translated. At question time, he translated their questions for me.

There was one young man during question time who rose up and said, "Sir, I sat down here and you have been talking for three hours. All the time I did not hear anything, I did not understand anything."

The reason he did not hear anything was that the whole time he had an iPod in his pocket, headphones in his ears and he was listening to music. Those sitting around him knew what he was doing and they all burst into laughter.

One of the leaders of our group had also noticed this, and he got angry. He said, "How can you plug your ears and listen to that music and then turn around and blame us because you didn't hear anything."

I said, "It's okay. He is alright."

So I said to the man, "It is unfortunate that you did not hear anything. So tomorrow when we meet again, come, and leave those things at home. When you come without those plugs in your ears, you will hear everything." They all laughed. He stayed for three hours, perhaps to get the meal. But he also came back the next day and was among those who were baptized on the Sunday.

Good humor will stand you in good stead. In stumping you get to a point where you have to be humorous, as Mark Prophet used to be. In the middle of a very serious teaching, Mark would sometimes slot in something to make you chuckle. Sometimes you have to ask a question that will encourage them to respond, maybe with some humor in it. So you keep them going.

When I saw those thousand people at our lecture, I could see that many were in pain. The people of Sierra Leone have not overcome all the trauma of the war. It stays with them. Even those who did not suffer injuries themselves still recall what they saw. They also recall the ordeal of running from their homes and spending months in the bush.

When you look at these people and you see the pain in the heart, how do you help these souls to find healing? By leading them to the point of forgiveness. But this is a very, very difficult task.

Some of those who committed these atrocities were neighbors. An individual has been living in this area as a friend and neighbor, now suddenly he returns, he holds a weapon and he is doing all of these things. Worst of all, after the hostilities are over, he comes to live in the same area again. When you see him, you recall everything that happened. How do you forgive such a person? How do you close your eyes to this? How do you live side by side?

So ministering to the people, particularly in Koidu City, which was the epicenter of the civil war, takes real guidance from the Lord Maha Chohan and the Holy Spirit.

I always look at the faces of the people. You can read from their faces what is in their hearts. Having experienced all of that trauma, they need and there is a longing in their hearts for something of the masters' teaching that will liberate their souls. And to come to the point of forgiving, they must understand why they have to forgive.

To get them to that point, if you are ministering to people who have seen so much pain, it is not helpful to refer to the past. You speak about what you think is the ideal situation. You acknowledge that this has been set aside and something else has replaced it. That other thing is the result of a lot of unwanted events that we have seen. You lightly touch on that, so they know that you are aware of what they have been through. And then you go on. We spoke with them about karma. With such people you also need humor and you must be helpful with their needs. You need a great deal of patience to deal with them.

Part of my approach was to try to understand what had led them to this state of affairs. It all originated in greed for the diamonds that are mined in the eastern part of the country. I analyzed all of this before I went. I knew they had been through a terrible war. But until I arrived there, I did not know the extent of the injury they went through, the harm and the trauma. Before I left I did much work at my altar. I prayed for forgiveness, for the binding of the greed, and for the souls of those involved to be healed.

The people did not just come for the food for their stomachs but also for spiritual sustenance. They had a very great hunger. If it was only for the food, they would not have returned for the service on the Sunday.

On that day we did not have food, and I did not expect a large number. But they came. We baptized about fifty people. The house and the compound where we met were full and people were outside. We had about a hundred all together, and all of them were there because they wanted to pursue the teachings. We formed a committee to take care of the group.

There is really the need for them to get the basic down-to-earth teaching. Alfred has written saying that the number of those who are coming for the teachings is increasing daily, and these are not ones who are coming for food. They want the teachings. We have to go back. But the road is so bad, and in the rainy season it is not possible to travel at all.

Mother said that the people of Africa are down-to-earth people. They live with the Holy Spirit. These are natural men and women, simple, beautiful hearts, kind to one another. But once the fallen ones get in, everything is turned upside down.

Chapter 44

The Devil Departs for a Season

One time a friend of mine suffered a very difficult situation of opposition. I told him, "Don't worry about what they did. Focus on your heart and on your mission." I realized that he had to take his attention away from what happened, because that would be a trap. This is what I would say to anyone in a similar situation.

When these tests come, they make you strong, but you can only be strong when you're focused on your objective. The question is, "What am I doing here?" And you answer, saying, "I am here because of my purpose in life, my mission."

When you establish a purpose for your life, why you are here, all those other things are merely attempts to sidetrack you. They don't matter.

Fighting back against those who want to draw you down is not what you want to give to the world. That's not why you're here. You are here because you want to share your knowledge or experience, you want to serve the people, you want the people to benefit from what you know. If there is someone standing there who doesn't approve of what you are giving in your service to life, that is his or her business. It is not yours.

There might be reactions from people to almost anything you might do. You can defeat them by being focused on your mission, the purpose for which you did what you did. If you are focused on that, forget them. You cannot stop them from reacting. But you can always put them to shame when you stand by the truth that you know and are acting on. The safest and surest way of getting out from under such a burden is to be focused on what you know in your heart is the right thing. That's all.

The scriptures tell the story about the blind man who was healed by Jesus. When the Jewish elders were trying to coerce him to say something against Jesus, he said, "If he is the devil, I do not know. If he is the son of Beelzebub, I do not know. If he is any of the things you are saying about him, I do not know. There is only one thing I know, that I was blind and now I see, and the source of my seeing is this man. That's all I know. Whoever you think he is, this is not my business. I don't know." That was a beautiful response to the Sanhedrin, to the devils who were plotting and planning against him.

When you are engaged in the work God has given you, you have more important things to do than to be swept away by the human nonsense. If your service is really helping people, this is far more important for the soul, it is far more pleasing to God, it far outweighs the nonsense that the jealous ones would want to place in your way. So it is important always to think of the positive things you are doing to help others. Don't even give one ear to what the jealous ones would want to do or say.

However, it is important to remember that you should not lose sight of them. Don't lose sight of the fact that every step you take they might be following two steps behind, looking for a way to trip you up. So make sure that the steps you take are sure, that where you place your feet is very firm ground. It is extremely important.

It is always important not to lose your guard. This is important in the physical, but even before that it must begin with prayer. We can ask each day that any negative energy that

217

may be sent to us be turned back—whether we are aware of it or not. Because if you don't stop doing good and showing kindness to others, seeking to bring peace and harmony to people's lives, those who are jealous will not stop sending those negative energies your way. Life is always complex and it is a battle. Every day is a fight. The fallen ones never give up.

My mind goes to the Bible, the New Testament, where it speaks about the temptation of Jesus. The devil showed him all the world, the beauty and glory of the world. And he said, "If you will bow down to me, all of this will be yours."

The Master turned to him and rebuked him. And then the Bible records that the devil "departed from him for a season."

I have never forgotten that statement. The devil left him for a while—not forever, not for good, but for a season. And the evil one has continued over the centuries and over the millennia, tempting, manipulating. The dark ones continue to plot and plan. The devil may leave you for a while. But the devil did not leave Jesus alone for good until he had won his final victory. Until then, he only left him for a while. It is the same for us.

You see in so many experiences in life the resilience of the dark ones, their determination not to let go until they have achieved what they set out to do. Fortunately, when they think that they have reached their goal, that is when the judgment comes. And be sure it will come. We can talk to the masters, tell them what has happened—as the old lady in Kumasi did. And the scriptures teach us to do this.

In the Acts of the Apostles, when the Jewish elders were harassing the disciples, they had arrested Peter. His colleagues certainly did not sit with arms folded while their colleague was in prison. The rest of the disciples went to the upper room and they were praying, as it says in the Book of Acts, "without ceasing."

This is the prayer that I hear them offering: "Lord, you sent your son to us. He taught us. Now he has left. We, the disciples, are here following his teachings and carrying out the good works that he asked us to do. And now, Lord, see how these people have moved to harass us as we seek to fulfill his commandments. And so, Lord, we pray: Raise up your hand and deliver us."

I love that prayer. It is naming the names, putting things in chronological order, so that the hosts of light would know what was the reason for making the request for assistance. I believe that is the way we should make our approach to the Science of the Spoken Word. This is always the way I make my complaint to the Lords of Life when there is a problem that needs to be addressed.

When we keep silent, when we do not pray, nothing happens. It is when we open our mouths and let out our feelings to the higher powers, it is when we pray fervently that the response must come. That's how you deal with injustice. And I always counsel people to spell it out.

In the Methodist Church, they used to pray like this, "Lord, you know everything. You know our needs. So help us."

I said, "My God, that's not scientific!" Be specific. Yes, God knows our needs, but he wants us to spell out our needs. If it's a telephone you need, tell him, "I need a telephone." If someone is taking a bottle and hitting your head, tell the masters, tell the Lord, "Someone is taking a bottle and hitting my head!" If you know the source of a problem, report it to the hosts of light.

When I am dealing with difficulties, I sit on my chair at my altar, I look at Maitreya, and I say, "Lord, you see what is happening. I will not call it injustice, because you know how to label it. But we are uncomfortable with this situation. This individual is doing this and this and this, and I'm not comfortable with it. I bring it to you to adjudicate this issue. I surrender it to you. It is your work I'm doing. It is because of you that

I am here, and this is what I have met in the exercise of your command. So it's up to you."

It is more than a prayer. It is a conversation. And we must name names. Otherwise, the tentacles will spread. We must be specific in our prayers when we know that a particular individual is the source of a problem. If we don't name names in our calls, we give the angels an unnecessary duty.

We are simply here as laborers in the vineyard of the Lord, and what we have observed is what we place before the masters. Whether they, the masters, should correct it or not is their business, not ours. Our business is to point out the problem.

So I will talk to Maitreya and ask him to deal with the problem, because as human beings, when we approach things on our level, sometimes we get emotional. Maitreya can look at it with different eyes, a different perspective than I would. I trust him.

Once you know the source of the problem, half of the victory is won. Each night before you go to sleep, talk to Maitreya, tell him the problems that you are having and ask him to take care of them all. See what he will do with them and how he will handle them. Wrongdoing is not an archetype of perfection. Don't place it before people. Don't talk about it. Just take it to the altar. Send it to the only Source.

Those who do the works of darkness stand on the wrong premise. The platform upon which they are launching their whole endeavor is not sound, and it will collapse under their feet. But the point is that now they hold temporal power and they think the way to use that power is to make life uncomfortable for the lightbearers.

Don't talk back to them. Go to your altar and speak. We do not know, but the Lord knows all. So we tell him. Let the mind of God adjudicate the issue.

Chapter 45

Those Who Leave the Path

People leave the spiritual path for many different reasons. Sometimes the reason can be found in the motive for the individual taking up the spiritual path in the first place.

There was a man who became a Keeper of the Flame in Ghana who worked at the post office in the engineering section at the university. He seemed so happy with the teachings and he used to be very regular in attending meetings. Then for some time we didn't see him.

I went to visit him at his workplace, and I asked him, "We are not seeing you these days. What's the problem?"

He said, "Oh, I have gone back to the Methodist Church."

I said, "Why?"

He was forthright with me. He said, "I came in there with an expectation. I had some problems, and I was expecting a miracle. That's why I came. But I have been there for several months and I haven't seen any improvement in the situation. That's why I have gone back to the Methodist Church."

I said, "But you did not tell me that you had this motive for coming to us. If we had known, we could have organized prayers for this particular problem." But he didn't tell us. So he had gone back to the Methodist Church.

"Well, it's fine that you have gone back," I said. "I was in the Methodist Church, and I pulled out and came to the

Summit. So if you were here and you have gone back to the Methodist Church, no problem." That was it.

People come in with different motives, different expectations, and if their expectations are not fulfilled, then they pull back. This man had difficulties in his life, as does everyone. And in expecting that being on the spiritual path he would have deliverance, he was not wrong. He was being truthful about his motives.

But people miss the mark because the spiritual path is not meant for material improvement. It is meant for the development of the soul, the inner man. The problem is ignorance and a lack of the proper understanding of what is involved on the path.

Some people leave the path because they find it difficult. At one time four of my own children came into the teaching. They knew the decrees, because we had been praying the decrees in the home. But after some time, they would not come to services any more. I asked them, "Why are you people sliding back, you are not coming?"

They said, "Papa, the Summit is difficult."

"How is it difficult?"

"You can't sit for one hour or two hours, just decreeing. It's too difficult. If we want to go to the Methodist Church on Sunday, we just get dressed up, get a taxi, go to church. We sing some hymns. We listen to a sermon. After a couple of hours, they close and we come home. This couple of hours in the Summit, you are decreeing. It's too difficult." So they found the effort and the discipline inherent in the path to be difficult.

All kinds of people will walk in the door of your church. They may stay for a couple of months and leave. Or they may be somebody who is very sincere who will persevere. You can't tell at the beginning which ones will stay, and they all need to have a good introduction to the path. You need to have the patience to take them through a systematic education and sharing of information about the teachings.

What I have found is that even if you set up a study group, if there is not a planned program for studying the teachings, the members will soon leave. But if you study the teachings in addition to the decrees, then people will stay and the group will grow. I always recommend that new study groups take up first *The Science of the Spoken Word* and study it systematically, from page to page. When they have finished this book, they will have imbibed some knowledge of the teachings. And when they have that understanding, it helps them.

I have also found in Africa that it is important to study the Bible. Whether we like it or not, the Bible is the basic spiritual book of all the churches. The teachings make many references to the Bible, and the masters have much to say about what has been written in the Bible. When people hear this understanding, it wakes them up: "Oh, I see. Everything that they are teaching is in the Bible. It is all there, but this is the real meaning of it."

I remember some years back, I preached a sermon at King Arthur's Court, the main chapel at headquarters. Someone came to me afterwards and said, "Reverend Paul, when you come to preach, you make the Bible become alive." I pick a text from the Bible and explain what the masters have said about what is in the Bible. It does help.

In fact, in all my outreach programs in Africa, I always include in my advertisements and announcements, "Bring your Bibles with you." Sometimes the fundamentalist Christians come intending to cause some trouble. But I will be well prepared to discuss the issues they want to raise. Particularly when I was doing the lecture "Karma and Reincarnation—the Missing Link in Christianity," I took the trouble to research all the Bible texts related to this subject.

In a lecture, when I want to speak about a particular text,

I ask the audience, "Please, will someone open their Bible and read this verse." So they are involved. They are listening. And then I explain what the masters have said about this verse. So by the time I end the lecture, people know that this is not some strange teaching we are giving that we have made up, but it is what is in their own Bible—but now they have the real, Holy Spirit interpretation of what they are holding in their hands.

I feel very sad for people when they leave the path. I feel sad because if they have a problem, they have come to the path that will give the solution to that problem—but they have left the path and run away. But I also feel hopeful that one day they will come back to the path, if they really want their freedom.

There is also another side to this equation. When Mother came to Ghana, a group came from Nigeria to see her. There was a woman in this group who was mentally disturbed. Sometimes she would be fine—she would come in and decree, and there was no problem. Then suddenly she would start behaving in a very abnormal way.

We saw that she was so enthusiastic. She came to all the services and church activities, she supported the church financially. But then at times she got into a state of mind where her behavior was abnormal.

We told Mother about her, and we were hoping that Mother would make calls for her so that she could be delivered of this problem. However, Mother said, "This is not the path for her. In this embodiment she has lost the opportunity to pursue this path." So we also know that this path is not for everyone. Jesus did not heal all those who came to him.

Sometimes when a person leaves the path, it may mean he or she will not take it up again in this embodiment. But I am always hopeful that the opportunity will come again, even if it is in their next life. Their time is postponed. That is all.

Chapter 46

The Ones Who Bite and Blow

I do not know if this is so in other nations, but in Africa when one wants to launch out to share the word of life as it is given by the ascended masters, one has to be extremely aware that the forces of darkness do not like the light of truth to be shared with the people, and they will always react. These dark ones come in various guises.

When you look out onto the street and you haven't ventured out, you will think that all is quiet and calm and peaceful. But when you get out there—when you, as it were, take the fight to their court—then they can bite in various forms. You become acutely aware that there are serpents who continue in their hatred against the light. And when they openly attack and find that they cannot achieve their purpose, then they may go behind the scenes and attempt witchcraft and black magic against us.

The knowledge that the light always defends the truth is that which gives courage and supreme certainty in the assurance that victory really always belongs to God and to the faithful. When we pursue the work of the Brotherhood with education and commitment and trust, the Brotherhood will always protect us, they will always reveal to us what is happening.

Of course, not every negative thing that happens is an attack. We also deal with returning karma. Mother's teaching is that if you have a problem in your physical body, when it is on the left side, it is generally an attack, it is a negative force attacking from outside of you. When it happens on the right side, it is more often your returning karma.

Bearing that in mind, when I have a problem, I take it to the altar and make my calls. I appeal to the Brotherhood. I go to Cyclopea, the Elohim of the fifth ray, and ask for the vision of the source to be revealed. Always my mind is shifted suddenly to something or someone, and what comes to mind is almost invariably the source of the problem. Then I increase my decrees on that particular cause.

I also remember what Lanello said, "When you make your calls and the problem seems to intensify, that is all the more reason to increase your calls. More will be revealed and more will be dealt with." I find that to be extremely true.

The masters have their own ways of prompting the student as to the cause or the source of opposition and how to deal with it. It all depends on one's closer walk, one's commitment and faithfulness in walking with the Brotherhood. It is like an agreement you have with the masters.

I walk in the world almost blind-eyed. So I say to the masters, "You want me to intensify the light, to do the works of the light, to share the light with men, to tell men that there is a way out of what we are experiencing on earth. But I am a blind man, as it were, and you are the ones with the eyes and the vision. So if it is in your interest that I should go out to share the little I know with others, then it must be in your interest to give me the guidance to protect that work."

That is the kind of bargain that I have with the masters. And they always win. The Brotherhood will not leave the one they send out unprotected and unguarded, and they always give the vision, the direction. What I call the tragedy in this kind of agreement is ourselves. As Saint Germain says, the unknown factor in the equation is man. How well do we keep our part of the agreement? I know that as far as the Brotherhood is concerned, no matter what, they will not turn their back on us.

Sometimes the opposition comes from unexpected sources. I have grown to realize that people have permanent interests, but they do not have permanent enemies. At a distance, people may seem to be fine, they are laughing, and the impression you get is that they are nice. But when you draw closer and step on their interests, then they turn to attack. We have a saying in Africa, "The crab also coughs, but if you are far from the river you will not hear." From far-off they are nice, they smile, they create a very good impression, but when you draw closer, you seem to step on their feet and they will bite.

There is another saying, "They bite and then they blow." They will bite and it will be painful, and then to cool it off, to take away the pain, they blow on the bite. You may realize they have bitten, but because they blow on it, you think that it was unintentional. You say, "Oh, he has bitten. But look at what he is doing now. He could not have meant it."

But the essential point is that they have bitten. That's what they had in mind. It was premeditated action.

It takes the wisdom of the Mother to discern what is behind the laughter of the wicked.

Chapter 47

The Legions Are Gathering

One time when I visited the Inner Retreat, Gene Vosseler said that there was a lady who wanted to see me. He mentioned her name, Evelyn Dykman, but I did not know who she was. Gene said he would take me to see her. So Gene, his wife, Wanda, and I went to Livingston to visit Evelyn.

We stopped the car, we went in, and Gene and Wanda said they would come back for me later. Evelyn was there, an elderly woman. I had never met her before. But Evelyn said to me, "Oh, Paul, I have been waiting for you for a long time."

Evelyn spoke about so many things that afternoon. She spoke about her friend, Ruth Hawkins, who had passed on some years earlier. Ruth was the twin flame of Paul the Venetian, and she had made her ascension and rejoined him. She spoke about living in the house where Ruth had lived. She had been with Ruth up until the end, and Ruth's children asked her not to leave after the passing of their mother.

After Ruth's cremation, Evelyn had received the ashes, and she still had them in the house. They had not been dispersed. One day Paul the Venetian had appeared to Evelyn and asked her, "Why is it that you don't want my twin flame to join me? The ashes should be placed in the heart of the Inner Retreat." Evelyn had told this to a friend who was a staff member, but he had not done it.

When I returned to the Ranch, I went to see this staff member and told him what Evelyn had told me. I said, "If what she says is true, this is something that is very important. Please go and see her, get the ashes and take them to the heart of the Inner Retreat." The following year when I visited, the ashes had been scattered. So the request was fulfilled.

Before I left visiting Evelyn, she stated again, "I have been waiting for you for a long time."

And then she said something very interesting: "Don't you know that the legions are gathering?"

I had always believed that, like many others, I was a part of a team that had come for the purpose. So when Evelyn said this, I was not surprised. I felt happy within. It was a confirmation to my mind and soul of an inner awareness of being part of a team that had some specific assignment to fulfill. And now the time is approaching when we should prepare to go back home.

That's the feeling I had. The legions are gathering and they are all heading towards home.

Chapter 48

Helios

One time when I was home in Ghana, I received a phone call from a Keeper of the Flame who lived in London, asking me to go there to officiate at her wedding.

I said, "What? I am in Ghana ministering to Africa. London is not part of my territory. Besides, flying from America to London is shorter and easier. Why don't you call the Ranch and ask them to send someone over?"

She said, "No, you have to come. I prayed to El Morya about who should be invited to officiate at the wedding, and it was your name that was given me."

She and her parents had been my friends, and she had been in Ghana as a member of the Ghana group, so I could not refuse. "Okay. I will come provided you make the travel arrangements for me."

So I traveled from Kumasi to Accra and went to the British High Commission to apply for my visa. They gave me a date to come back, and I returned to Kumasi. A few days later, I was walking down the street and my phone rang. I was needed at the British High Commission immediately to get my visa. I returned home and told my wife, "I am going to Accra and I will be back later today."

I got in my car, and I think I was speeding because I wanted to do the journey in about three hours. (Because of the nature of the road, it usually takes four or five.) While I drove, I was really calling on Morya, singing and decreeing to him, and I had tears coming down my face as I made these calls. I don't fully understand what was happening on that journey, but I was singing, praying, crying and speeding down the road.

After about fifty miles, I was stopped at a police barrier. The policeman said, "I have a colleague here who needs to go to Accra. Would you take him with you?"

I said, "Okay. Let him jump in."

I had my radio cassette player on the passenger's seat in the front and I was playing tapes of decrees and songs, so I had the policeman sit in the back. He sat very straight, as if he was on duty. He did not move. I kept on driving with the tapes running. He asked me, "Sir, you are driving alone? Are you not afraid?"

I said, "The car is full."

He said, "What?"

I said, "The car is full. I had to give an excuse to some other people before you jumped in."

He didn't dare ask me, "Where are the people?" But I think he understood somehow that I was praying and that the car was full of angels.

We drove straight to the British High Commission in Accra, but when we got there we found they had closed for the day. My ticket was to fly out of Accra at eight o'clock the following evening on British Airways, and I still didn't have a visa.

I went to my home in Accra and called the High Commission the following morning. They said to come down at two o'clock. So I went there to pick up my passport and visa, and then went back to my place in Accra to pack. By six o'clock I was at the airport. I had been planning to return to Kumasi to prepare for the trip, but because of the delay with the visa, all I had was the clothes I was wearing and a very few items I had in Accra. All my things were still in Kumasi.

I arrived in London around seven o'clock the next morning. The lady at whose wedding I was to officiate met me at the airport and took me to her home, and I stayed there. The wedding was a couple of days later at Canterbury.

After the wedding I had an invitation from another minister who was in Norway at that time to take part in a public outreach he was organizing. While I was in London pondering over this invitation, a lot of things came to my mind.

I was thinking about how it came about that I was there in England, doing this wedding. It occurred to me that I was the only ordained minister in Africa. If something should happen to me, how would they train someone to replace me? How would the church activities go on? Then I said to myself, "Let me ask permission from headquarters so that we can train a few people in Ghana for the ministry. In case anything happens we will have some people on hand to carry on the masters' work." I had the idea that I should travel to headquarters to try to arrange this.

I was also thinking of the circumstances by which I got to London. First I had told my wife I was going to see the British High Commission in Accra, only for me to tell her the next day that I was getting on the plane to go to London. I did not even leave any money for her and my family. How were they even going to eat?

And here I was in London, penniless and with these clothes that normally one would not take to travel. I had left Ghana with just my return air ticket, not even an extra pound in my pocket. Now I was thinking of going to Norway and even to America? Was I really on the right track? Or was there something wrong with me? Was I mad to be here in such circumstances and thinking of such things? I had an intense desire to know whether everything I was thinking was just an illusion or not.

It was evening. I went to stand at a window looking west. The sun had set and I remembered the prayer that Mother had made to Helios in the Heart of the Inner Retreat when we were there in 1981.

So I made my calls to Helios and I repeated the decrees to Helios and Vesta over and over again. Then, lo and behold, the sun that had set came up again, brightly shining. I put my hands on my head and I said, "O God, what have I asked for?" And there were tears flowing, soaking my shirt. I went down on my knees at the window and I said, "Helios, if I have done something wrong, please forgive me."

I heard, in my mind, the Great One saying, "No, you have done nothing wrong. You can call on me any time. You are my friend."

I felt greatly relieved, because I had really felt that I was going mad to be there in such circumstances. But when I saw the sign of the sun, I knew I was on the right course, it was part of the plan, the arrangement of the Brotherhood.

When my niece came home I told her what had happened. Then I sat down with her and wrote out a plan and a proposal for training ministers in Ghana. I called the Inner Retreat and said I was in Britain. It was easier to get to Montana from there, and could I come? They agreed and sent an invitation letter to the American Embassy for my visa.

I went to Norway and took part in the seminar there, and when I returned to London, I submitted my papers to the American Embassy. It was wonderful. They took just three days to issue my visa. I did not even have to go there, they sent it by courier.

I told my niece that I did not have the money for the air ticket. She told one of the members of the London group, and this person provided the ticket. That ticket took me to America and brought me back to London. I already had my return ticket to Ghana.

It was really a miracle the way all these arrangements worked out. And that also reassured me that things were okay.

Many times when my niece speaks with me from London, she will say, "Papa, I stood at your window." She remembers that place where I saw the run rise again as my window.

I will say to her, "Well, if you are standing at my window, call to Helios and Vesta. They will answer you."

Decree to Helios and Vesta

Helios and Vesta!
Helios and Vesta!
Helios and Vesta!
Let the Light flow into my being!
Let the Light expand in the center of my heart!
Let the Light expand in the center of the earth
And let the earth be transformed into the new day!

Salutation to the Sun

O mighty Presence of God, I AM, in and behind the Sun:
I welcome thy Light, which floods all the earth,
into my life, into my mind, into my spirit, into my soul.
Radiate and blaze forth thy Light!
Break the bonds of darkness and superstition!
Charge me with the great clearness
of thy white fire radiance!
I AM thy child, and each day I shall become
more of thy manifestation!

Chapter 49

Training Ministers for Africa

I arrived at the Inner Retreat in May 2001 having traveled from Ghana to Britain and Norway with only two shirts and two pairs of trousers. When I got there I submitted my proposal for setting up the ministerial training program. At the beginning, I had in mind only Ghana, but when I discussed this with the Office of Ministry we realized that it should cover the whole of Africa.

The ministerial trainees from the program at headquarters were graduating and being commissioned at the July conference that year, so I got involved in that, which was a joyful experience. This was the same year that I happened to be, by the masters' grace, appointed the regional minister for Africa. So it was a double joy, going out as the regional minister for the continent and having the opportunity to set up the ministerial training program for the continent.

When I arrived back in Ghana at the end of July, I had to lay the groundwork for the training. One of the members of the church, Dr. Edzii, had been registrar of the University of Ghana, Legon, and I asked him to be the registrar for our program. I also asked Rev. Donkoh to help. We wrote to South Africa, to Nigeria and to the Ghana church telling them about the program and inviting those who felt that they wanted a career in the ministry to come forward.

Rev. Paul Kyei, Rev. Frances MacPherson and Rev. Kenneth Frazier at the first ministerial training class in Accra, May 2003

People applied from all three countries, twenty-six in total. We called each of them for an interview. One we found was not 100% with Church Universal and Triumphant, had other allegiances and was still tied to another organization. For one, his knowledge of the teachings was not up to what we expected. One was not accepted because his command of the English language was not good enough. There were twenty-two who began the program.

The first session was in May 2003. Rev. Frances Mac-Pherson and Rev. Kenneth Frazier came from America to teach. Kenneth and his wife, Rev. Bonita, came to teach in subsequent years.

The course was supposed to run for three years, but there was a problem at the beginning with the grading of the students' papers. Dr. Edzii and Rev. Donkoh used a different grading system from what Frances was expecting. Kenneth thought the standard of the students' work was very high, but the way their papers were graded did not do justice to their work. Frances asked the students to do additional work, and the program ended up taking five years in total.

Five of the students who started the program did not graduate. Two were not submitting their assignments, so I had to write to them to ask them to either do what was required or withdraw honorably from the program. Another student had an issue bordering on a mental health problem, and she was also asked to withdraw from the program and seek the help of a counselor.

Sadly, one of the students from Nigeria was murdered in Lagos. He came to the first intensive, but then we never heard from him after that. The members in Nigeria went looking for him. They found out what had happened to him, but they never found out who killed him or why.

Another student died in Ghana. He was taken ill for just a day or two and he passed on suddenly. He had been in training at one time to become a Catholic priest, and he had visited the Vatican. But he told me that he did not like what he had seen in the Catholic ministry, so he withdrew from the Catholic Church. It hurt them very much, because he was very intelligent, very promising. It was a great loss for us when he died.

The graduation ceremony for the students was in 2008, and in 2009 we held the commissioning ceremony for twelve lay ministers and two lay sisters. Since their commissioning the lay ministers and lay sisters have been serving in their various countries. They have been actively involved in outreach—actually, the word *outreach* does not appeal to me. I prefer to use Mother's term, *stumping*. They are also leading services and helping in many ways.

We are grateful to the Brotherhood for the commitment of these students. If all things go well, some of them will soon be ordained ministers. Then Paul can have a little corner to sit and relax a bit more!

Rev. Paul Kyei presiding at the ceremony
for commissioning lay ministers in 2009

The new lay ministers and lay sisters after their commissioning

Chapter 50

A Minister's Heart

A role of leadership always comes with many challenges. This is even more so with a role of spiritual leadership, because of the many expectations people have of a minister or spiritual leader.

I think that there is a clear path for anyone who would want to succeed in any responsibility given to him or her. First and foremost is to study the rules and the regulations, the guidelines and directions pertaining to that responsibility. For service in a church, the foundation will be the bylaws or the constitution of the church. Every other rule or guidance pertaining to any organization in the church has its root in these, and they should be studied very carefully.

The next thing for someone newly appointed is to work out how to fulfill the particular assignments given by that office. Can he implement them all with the means already at hand, or does he need to innovate, fashion new tools, figure out how he is going to do it? He should be prepared to adapt and change, because it is when you begin to implement a policy that you see the loopholes and the shortcomings that require changes.

Who are the people who should help him fulfill the mandate of that office? Are the people mandated by the rules and the existing structure adequate for the task? Or does he need to look for others who have the expertise to make it happen. In either case, the leader should resolve within that he will give his fullest cooperation and cultivate a mutual trust with each one who is to help him.

Looking back on my own experience, I realize that when you have a love for the particular thing you are expected to do, you can do it better. If you love to do it, you do it better than when you approach a task half-heartedly or reluctantly. So it is important to cultivate that love.

The same is true for those who are assisting you. You often achieve better results when you explain the need and ask for volunteers rather than just asking someone to do a task. If someone offers voluntarily to do a job, "This is what I would like to do to help," he will do it better than someone who has just been prevailed upon to do it.

When it comes to spiritual offices, there is the need to go the extra mile. This can become quite demanding, because people have certain expectations of spiritual leaders. You cannot function as a minister in the same way you would as a managing director of a corporation. When the attitude of those around you is cordial and cooperative, you are encouraged to give more of yourself. But when there is hostility, you may feel compelled to withdraw—it is a natural tendency. But people expect more of a spiritual leader. They expect that the minister will always be there for them, even when they, themselves, are not behaving well. The minister should try to minister to all equally, not to treat people differently based on personal preferences. Openness and transparency are essential.

Every human being has faults. It can be very difficult, and even painful, when you come face to face with the low side of a person's character. However, these are the things that happen on the path. You don't have to dwell on them. Sometimes you have to ignore them completely. But even then, you must let them be a teacher unto you. You may not act on what you see, but you don't forget that it is part of the human character that may, if allowed, obstruct your path.

I have an elderly friend in Kumasi who says, "The elder is always to be pitied." In our culture, whenever there is a problem, something that is not right in the family or the home, a person brings this to the elder to resolve. People may even create problems and bring them to the elder to resolve.

When you are in a new office, there are always cross-currents of energy, each one trying to see what level of control he or she may have. The whole issue of your role and what you get involved with has to be approached with great care and circumspection, because things can easily become so muddy when you become enmeshed in areas where you should not.

As a leader, it is important to know what is your responsibility and what is not. If you study the rules and the constitution defining your office, you will see where the line of your responsibility begins and where it ends, and you will realize that there are certain areas where it is not helpful to step in. Not only is it not helpful, but it will lower the status of the office to get involved. You have the responsibility to protect the dignity of your office.

There is a natural tendency to want to please others, to impress them, and therein lies slippery ground. Be compassionate and seek to serve, but the aim should be that the people you serve should themselves become stronger and more capable of serving in their own right.

Do not feel the worth of your service is weighed only in great accomplishments. Do little things as God gives you opportunity. Little things often have within themselves the inclination to a higher way that may be imparted to others.

The minister or spiritual leader must see himself always as a student, perpetually learning. It is necessary to continually study what the masters and messengers have given. The process of learning also comes through the people around the leader and from the job itself.

A minister must be able to hold confidential that which he hears from others. If he thinks there is the need to share that information, he must first ask the person who gave it if he has any objection to it being shared with others. Otherwise it is privileged. If he cannot hold these things in his heart, others will shy away from him and he will lose a lot of vital information. Also, people will not confide in him and he will lose the opportunity to provide counsel and spiritual assistance.

I always seek to remember that the people in my congregation are God's people. He knows how to handle them. He knows why he gave me the privilege to lead them—a kind of a shepherd boy leading the flock. I ask God to help me to lead effectively, to guide his own people.

At the same time, I do not lose sight of the possibility of negative energy coming not only from without but also from those within. The devil often comes in through one simple thing—jealousy. And one word from a fellow minister to a member of the community, a word which is not in support and praise of a colleague, but casting a slur on the integrity and the effort of that one, goes a long way to influence people in a negative way.

Bearing in mind you are always a servant of someone yourself, even when you are in a leadership role, you should always be very humble in that role. It is not a matter of telling people, "Do this and this and this." The true leader always relies on the one source, God, who gives the opportunity to lead his own people.

Saint Paul said, "All things are lawful unto me, but all things are not expedient." Some people in positions of leadership feel that they have the right, the freedom to think anything and to say anything that they want to say, forgetting that thinking anything and saying anything is not always helpful. You don't know if the person to whom you say something unhelpful may be the next person to be very important in your life. What you have said and what you have thought will be returned. And once the human mind grasps what has been said, how much damage has been done? We may talk of forgiveness, but how deep and sincere will forgiveness be?

Leading people is no easy task. I think it is the most difficult assignment in the world. You are leading people who have their own ways of thinking. They have been brought up with different backgrounds and the way they do things is different from what you know. What is needed is the willingness to try to understand. So in addition to humility, you need patience. Take the time to try to understand where people are coming from. If you remember this, you won't get angry with them.

If you don't listen to the other person, you will not know the real issues. You may think you have to apply the rules in a certain way. But forget about that. Don't think about what you are going to say, just listen to what the other person says. Then you may well say to yourself, "Oh, I did not understand. My approach should be to go this way—not what I had thought."

On a very few occasions, I have had to correct a member and apply some sanction. I think I have done so only on two occasions in all the years of my leadership in the community. In these situations I will sit and talk with the person. "You know this is what the situation is, this is what you did. As a community, we have our rules or norms that guide us. Do you think what you have done supports us or it does not? If not, what do you think you should do?"

So he himself will be the judge. He will likely realize that what he did was wrong. If he is sincere, he may well know what he should do to make amends. He may ask what I think, but if it comes from within him, he will really learn from the experience.

Sometimes I might say, "For the sake of the community and for a better example for others, we think it is good that you stay away for a few weeks. This will also be time for you to reflect."

That has happened on only two occasions that I recall. One was a staff member. I told him he was relieved of his staff duties for four weeks. The other was a member of the community who had a problem between him and his wife. He left her and he said he wanted to marry another girl. He was saying it was pressure from his family.

There are many instances of this in our country. For example, if a man marries a woman and she has difficulty bringing forth children, they don't blame the man, they always blame the woman. So the family will want the man to leave the woman and take on another wife, one who will bear a child.

There are also situations where the family wants the man to marry someone from his town. If he marries someone from a different place, they may try to force him to leave her and take another woman. This often means a great deal of trouble for the people involved.

This young man in our church had his wife and he had two children. His parents wanted him to marry another woman, someone from his home town. Instead of standing his ground, he yielded to that pressure. When it came to my notice, I called him. I said, "Well, my friend, as you are in this group, the reputation of the group rests on you. Don't think that I am the minister so I have the sole responsibility."

I asked him to look at the situation from the perspective of someone from outside the community: "You have two children with the woman. You don't just leave her. If you were someone outside the church observing what is happening, what would you feel about this? What would you think of our community? What would you think of a church where this is the kind of behavior that occurs?"

I asked him to take time off, to put things in their proper perspective, to settle the issues with the women involved and with his family, and then come back.

He was not happy at the beginning. He stayed away for quite some time, and after reflecting, going within, turning things over in his mind, he decided to go back to the Catholic Church, where he had been before. But after some more reflection, weighing what he had learned from the masters' teaching, he decided to come back to us again, and he is still here. He returned to his wife and children, and they are now living happily together.

Sometimes you come across issues like this that are very difficult. It is not a question of applying the law blindly. You review the situation with the person, you let the person take part fully in the discussion. Often the decision will come from him.

Sometimes I had to have the courage, the humility and the forthrightness to say, "I have made a decision. This is what I have decided, and it has to be so." But these occasions are rare.

In my role in the Methodist Church, I received training in preparation for entering the ministry. We had courses and some of the training was outside of Ghana. We learned that leadership is all based on the love you have for those for whom you have been given responsibility. If you love, then everything you do is love. You love the people you are to serve, and you are grateful to the one who gave you the responsibility. There is always the flow, there is the link.

Chapter 51

The Final Journey

In West Africa, funerals are very big occasions. Not only the family is involved, but also all of the extended family, friends and acquaintances. Funeral celebrations may last several days, and they can be very expensive. Some families even incur large debts to pay for a funeral, which can be a considerable burden for a widow and children—yet people feel that this is what is expected of them.

In earlier days, there were few mortuaries and morgues in our country. When a person died, the body had to be buried within twenty-four hours. Now that there are many mortuaries in the hospital system, the body can remain unburied for a month or more, and this is not uncommon. Many people from Ghana live in other countries, and when the mother or father passes on, children outside the country would like to be there for the funeral, so the ceremony is delayed to a convenient time. It is nearly always a burial, since cremation is something that is not well accepted in Africa.

The masters have recommended cremation as the best way to dispose of a body after death. However, when members of our church request cremation, we often have opposition to it from members of the family.

One of the difficulties around cremation in our culture is that people think that burning a body is something that is done when someone is evil. I remember when one of our church members died at Dunkwa, which is close to Kumasi. They brought the body to Kumasi for the cremation and we went there for the service. A woman who had been in my Methodist bible class said to me, "Brother, what has this man done that he is to be burned?"

I said, "He has not done anything wrong." I explained to her that cremation is the best way of disposing of the body. I gave her the example of grave robbers, who dig up the graves of people who are newly buried to get the ornaments that people are buried with. These days you don't hear much of it. I guess the watchmen at the cemeteries are very serious with their duties now, but there used to be a lot of this. And it's not only the grave robbers. Sometimes people use parts of dead bodies, bones and other things, for black magic.

I said, "How would you like your body being dug out of the grave when your family has buried you? When the body is burned nothing is left of you here for the grave robbers. And it is the process of quickly saying goodbye to the body so the soul can be free to move on." This is the way I explained it to her.*

---

* Apart from these reasons, cremation also provides important spiritual benefits for the soul. Mark and Elizabeth Prophet explain this in their book *The Masters and the Spiritual Path:* "In order to facilitate the soul's transition to higher octaves, either to complete the requirements for the ascension or to enter into temple training for the next life, Serapis Bey has recommended that the physical body be placed on ice for a period of three days after death and that it then be cremated....

"Through this ancient ritual, the light in the heart of the physical atoms is released by the fire element, and the energy that was used to sustain the form is immediately returned to the heart of the God Presence.... Cremation eliminates the possibility of the form exercising dominion over the soul through what is called residual magnetism; for the records of the individual's thoughts and feelings do leave a residue of substance that creates a magnetic forcefield in the body even after interment, which tends to keep the soul earthbound.

"The passage of the soul to higher octaves is facilitated by the blessed fiery salamanders [nature spirits of the fire element], who consume not only the physical body but also that portion of untransmuted substance lodged within it.... When the physical form is not cremated, the pull of the records and of the residual magnetism within the forcefield of the body is so great that the soul usually remains in the lower astral levels between embodiments." [pp. 123, 124, 125]

"So, Brother, you want to tell me that you as you are sitting here, if you die, they are going to do the same thing to you?"

I said, "Sister, I am doing it to others, why wouldn't they do it to me?"

I looked at her face and I couldn't help but laugh. I could tell from the expression on her face that the thought of cremation was so repulsive to her mind.

Apart from the many benefits for the soul who has passed on, cremation avoids unnecessary expenses involved in burials. When a parent passes on, the children are obliged to provide the coffin, and these days it is really a burden. The family will want to have the most expensive coffin they can afford, something fitting to the man's standing in society. Yet this will just be buried in the ground. In a cremation the coffin is made of wawa, an inexpensive African wood that burns easily. So the cremation saves on the cost of the coffin.

But there is even some prejudice about this. Sometimes people will think that if you don't spend a lot of money on the funeral, you don't really feel sad that your relative is dead.

It is only recently, with members of esoteric organizations opting for cremation, that it has become more popular. Now even some individuals in orthodox churches are also choosing cremation. This is among educated people, however. Those who have not been to school do not choose it at all.*

Cremation is gaining popularity in Africa not only in Ghana. The present cremator in Accra, who uses firewood, was

---

* To those in Africa, I would say: Please make sure that you educate your family members well about the process of cremation and your desires after your death. If someone passes on and the family raises any objection, according to our custom family members are the ones who have the final say. If they object to cremation, the church will not litigate on this issue. We will be obliged to allow the matter to rest there. So if you prefer to be cremated rather than undergo burial of the body, arrange this with your family members ahead of time and ask them to respect your wishes. Fill out the cremation form and get a family member to witness the document so there will be no doubt about your intentions. —PKK

telling me that sometimes people will bring a body from the Ivory Coast just to be cremated in Ghana. So gradually it is spreading. Just recently one of our members told me that there are some people who are planning to build a complete gas-fired crematorium in Accra. It will be a very beautiful facility.

Something that has encouraged the growing popularity of cremation is that the local authorities are finding that it is difficult to find land in Accra for burials. The existing burial grounds are all full. So they are thinking of cremation to avoid the need for more land for cemeteries.

Another advantage of cremation is that there is absolutely no opportunity for black magic to be involved in any way. One of our members passed on earlier this year, and the family asked me to prepare to cremate his body because the dead man had a brother who indulged in black magic. The two of them did not get on, and they thought that if he were buried, the brother might tamper with the body. So I said we would do it.

They brought the body to our church on the day of the cremation. All the village people followed and came to the service. They were wailing on the ground. I said to them, "We don't do that in our church. If you had wanted to wail, you could have done that in the village. Here, no." So they stopped. We had a nice service for him, and then we went to the cemetery for the cremation. On Sunday morning they collected the ashes and scattered them in the sea.

The Monday following, the mother and the sisters came to my house in Accra. The mother was an old lady. She thanked me for doing this cremation. But there was one more thing she wanted me to know. She had a fetish idol, a small god, in her home. When her son died, she said to the idol, "You were here and you could not protect my son and he died, so I am leaving you."

She went to the church that her other children attended. She went to see the pastor and they came and collected the idol and they burned it. So now she is a Christian.

Usually we hold our cremation services on a Saturday morning. At 6 a.m. church members gather to give Astreas and violet flame decrees to cut free the soul of the one who has passed. We don't allow people who are not members of our church to enter until we have completed our spiritual work.

The body is brought to the church at seven o'clock. It is in the wawa coffin with Kente cloth draped over it. Kente cloth is a national attire, peculiar to Ghana, and the family members often wear clothing made out of the same cloth, often in the same style. The coffin is placed on stands in front of the altar. We take off the Kente and people can file past and view the body. This is traditional. We play classical music during the viewing.

At eight o'clock, we put the lid on the coffin and start the usual memorial service. We have an invocation by Mother, the candle lighting, and we welcome the people. We tell them the purpose of being there and explain the program, which includes prayers, songs and scripture readings. This is a service for family and friends, so it does not include decrees.

After the prayers we have a period for people to give their witnesses and tributes to the dead, no more than thirty minutes. If it is a church member, the church will give its tribute or eulogy, then the husband or wife, then the children, and then friends or colleagues who want to say something. We have a short sermon. We take a love offering, and whatever we collect goes to the family. The service is one-and-a-half to two hours.

Before the service ends, we perform the ritual that Mother has taught for withdrawing the light from the body. Two ministers stand by the body, one at the head and one at the feet, and they give the invocation for the light to be withdrawn. We want the congregation to see this ceremony and we explain what we are doing. Then we say we are going to the crematorium.

We get there around noon for the graveside service. The cremator has brought the coffin in his hearse. The fire is prepared but not lit. He arranges the funeral pyre so nicely. He learned how to do it from the Indian community. It is not very high.

The cremator has a special butter or margarine that he spreads over the wood, and he lights a little fire to the side. When we have completed the graveside service, we invite the children to come forward and put a torch to the funeral pyre. Each child is given a torch to light the pyre, if they want to do this. The fire is lit, we conclude with a prayer, we shake hands with all the family members, and we leave.

If there is a reception, we go there for a while for snacks, drinks and fellowship. That is not the concern of the church. We tell them it is their choice to have a reception or not.

Early next morning, between five and seven o'clock, a representative of the church, a representative of the family, and the cremator collect the ashes. If there is no other direction, they go to the sea and scatter the ashes there—it is not far away. They use a portion of the graveside prayer when the ashes are scattered. By the time they return, we will be holding our Sunday service, which begins at 10:30 a.m. This is a service that family, friends, co-workers and everyone who attended the previous day is invited to attend, as well as church members.

We pick a text and give a short sermon. We choose the message depending on who was there on Saturday and what would be most helpful for them. There are no further testimonies or eulogies at this service. The purpose is to say, "Thank you, O God, for giving us the life of our father, our brother, our sister, our mother."

Chapter 52

A Quiet Man

Dr. Ebenezer Adentwi Kofi Edzii was a member of Church Universal and Triumphant. He joined us in 1972, having come from the Methodist Church, as many of our members did, and he was baptized by Mark Prophet. He was the registrar of Ghana's premier university, the University of Ghana, Legon, Accra, for twenty-one years.* It was the first President of Ghana, Dr. Kwame Nkrumah, who took him from the government administration and brought him to the university as the registrar, and he served well. His doctorate was an honorary one conferred on him by the university.

Dr. Edzii was a quiet man. People said he was a strict disciplinarian, and this description fitted him. Perhaps this is not surprising, seeing that he had been a district commissioner in the colonial government.

This man was very independent. He did not join any organization. He was not even a member of any of the lodges that many of the educated people in our country join. So it was a great surprise to the university community when they found out that Dr. Edzii had become a member of Church Universal and Triumphant.

He had much wisdom and insight, so we valued and

---

* The University of Ghana follows the British system, where the head of the university's administration holds the title of registrar.

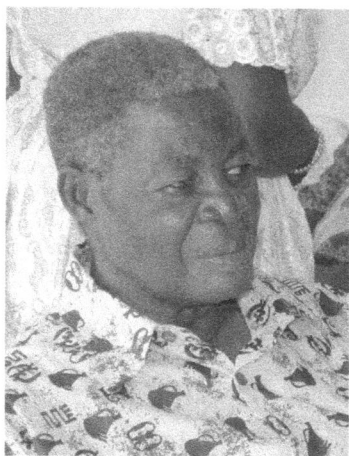

Dr. Ebenezer Edzii

treasured our association with him. When I took over as director of the church in Ghana in 1982 and the lay ministers had gone to Nigeria, I was left very much alone. I appointed Dr. Edzii to be on the board of the Church of Ghana at that time, and I valued his counsel very much. He served as vice-president of the Ghana church, and in later years he was also the chairman of the church growth committee.

In February 2003, we set up a regional board for all of Africa, and Dr. Edzii was instrumental in this. He was a lawyer and he drew up the constitution for this body as well as serving as a board member.

When we had the opportunity to set up the Ministerial Training Program in Africa, we thought that with his experience as a university lecturer and administrator, he would be the ideal person to serve as registrar for the program, and he willingly accepted this role.

Dr. Edzii celebrated his eighty-second birthday on February 2, 2010, and he passed on February 15. In later years, he was in and out of the hospital many times because of his age. However, we did not think it was time to say goodbye. So it was with surprise and great sadness that we received the announcement that he was gone. It was a very painful loss.

His son called me very early, around five o'clock in the morning, and gave me this news. I called Rev. Donkoh, and around eight o'clock we all met at his residence. The family was there. We were talking about where to bury him and other arrangements that had to be made. I did not know that he had signed a cremation form with the church, so I did not speak about this.

I went back to the church and the staff looked in our file cabinet and brought me Dr. Edzii's file. There was a sealed letter addressed to his family. I knew that this would have to be the form requesting that his body be cremated. He had signed the agreement confidentially. Two of his family members had witnessed it, he had sealed it in an envelope and asked our staff to put it in his file.

I called his house again and asked to speak to his widow. I said that Dr. Edzii had written something for us and I would like to meet again. It was a sealed letter and I would like to open it and read it for everybody to hear what was written. They summoned the family and we met the following morning. I gave the letter to Rev. Donkoh and asked him to open it and to read it.

This was Dr. Edzii's last confidential testament for the disposal of his remains after he passed. Donkoh read the entire document in English and then in the Fante dialect. I looked at all their faces. Then the elder of his family said, "Well, this man is a scholar, and the scholar has spoken in this letter. We cannot say anything about it. The tribe is there, and they have their customs, but this man is a family elder. So it will be fulfilled for him as he has wished."

I heaved a sigh of relief, because Edzii being an elderly person, aged 82 when he passed, it could be difficult. People often say, "From the time of our grandfathers up to now, when someone has died we don't do cremation. Why are we doing this now? It is not something that is done in our village." And there was no way we could go against the wishes of the family, regardless of what was in the will.

Even after hearing this letter, his family said that the agreement for cremation was provisional. They had to go to his town, summon all his family and hear their wishes. I said, "That's all right with the church, go ahead."

That was Saturday. They went to his town on Tuesday. It is a coastal town, a fishing town, and fishermen don't go to sea on Tuesday. It is a holiday for them, so everybody would be there when they had the family meeting.

The letter was read to the whole family. They saw that his younger brother had witnessed and signed the cremation letter. So they said again, "This man is a scholar, and we cannot dispute what he has written." I was so relieved when the family finally agreed to do the cremation.

Because of his prominent role at the university, Dr. Edzii was known by many people. When they heard that he was to be cremated, there was a mixture of surprise and uncertainty. Why would he ask for cremation? That was really something they wanted to see.

I told the family members, even though it seemed that everyone knew it would be a cremation, they should send special invitations to the university to remind them that he had passed on and let them know the program. We did not want to have anyone surprised on the day of the service.

We had done some radio and TV announcements and filed notices in the papers, so many people came. Our chapel was full and we erected tents in the yard with chairs for more people. People were even standing in the street outside the church. So we determined to seize the opportunity to let people know what cremation was. Thank God, the message was well received.

We had announced ahead of time that anyone who desired to offer a tribute at the service should contact the family so that they could be included in the program. However, on the day of the service many university professors said that they wanted to give a tribute. We said, "We are sorry, but you did not let us know in advance so we could put you on the program. We are going forward according to the program."

The man who succeeded Dr. Edzii as registrar of the university also asked to speak, and we told him the same thing. Probably he thought that because of his position he would be given preference, but I was sticking to the program and I wanted it to be on time. It was Emmanuel who drew my attention to the fact that he was the registrar, and he felt that he should be allowed to speak.

So after everybody had finished reading their tributes to the doctor, I called on the registrar. I said that there was no better person than the one who replaced Dr. Edzii as registrar to give the final tribute to him. When I had told him he could not speak, it had been a real concern for him, so when he got to the podium he said, "Thank you very much for allowing me to speak. I would have been carrying with me some bitterness against you if you had not allowed me to read my tribute. But I must apologize for not submitting it ahead of time." He said this in front of everyone, and then he gave his tribute.

I gave a brief sermon. I have forgotten the exact text that I chose, but it was on rejecting all that one could think of in life and deciding to take to the path. What did the doctor find in the teachings of the masters that made him leave the church that he belonged to in order to be here? When you think that this is not a very large congregation, what is it that he saw on the path of the teachings of the masters that made him say goodbye to his former place?

When I give a sermon, I take a text and then link it to life, to make it real for the people. It is quite a challenging thing to do, but it is very interesting when it is successful. I spoke for only ten minutes. Some of the people had come from the coast, fishermen and their families. They needed to hear the message in their own language. I gave a portion in English, a portion in

Akan, so that everyone there could go home with at least a word or a sentence.

The family later told Nada, my assistant, "Tell the Bishop we are grateful. We were expecting a long talk, as they do in the Methodist Church and other churches. But he did ten minutes, and those ten minutes were so loaded that we all felt satisfied."

After the memorial service, we conveyed the body from the chapel to the crematorium. Many of the people came for that service also.

When it was all over, one man I thought would be opposed to what had been done said to me, "Oh, this thing is beautiful. It is so simple and straightforward. Maybe one day I will opt for this." I was extremely happy and grateful to the masters. Even if he does not come forward to join us in any way, I hope that in his own private life he will choose cremation.

Chapter 53

Duty and Family

I have eight children. The first is Yaw Opong, a boy. He is a driver in Ghana. Paulina is a nurse in Montreal. Jonas works in a saw mill in Ghana. Isaac was with the Ghana Meteorological Agency and he is now a driver in Kumasi. He is the only one who is now with me in the teachings. Michael also works in a saw mill. My sixth child is a girl, Unity. She is a hotel receptionist. She is married to a police officer and they live in Accra. Jane is a teacher, and she lives in Montreal. Kwabena is a welder.

All of my children have African names, but they go by their English names. They are all married and have children of their own, my grandchildren. There are now twenty-nine grandchildren and six great-grandchildren.

My first grandchild was born September 12, 1976, the very day that Mother arrived in Ghana. I was in Accra meeting Mother, and I told her, "Mother, my first granddaughter was born today, and she is at my house." Mother named her Paula—that's how she received that name. Sadly, she died in 2003, at age 29. Her death was a great sorrow to me and the cause of one of the most severe initiations on my spiritual path.

I was very close to Paula. From the time that her mother gave birth, they were living with me in my house in Kumasi. She was literally born on my lap. She was with me all the years from kindergarten and all the way through high school. I paid for her education. I brought her down to Accra, found her a job in the University, and she worked there in the administration. She was living in my house. We were very close. But in our culture the mother's side has a lot of control over the children. She was given in marriage without even my prior knowledge or consent.

After she married, Paula moved to her husband's house, which was not far from where I lived in Accra. She had only one child, a very beautiful boy. He died in 2003. About two months later, Paula fell sick herself, and her husband took her to the hospital. After a while she passed on. I did not know what she died from. Even the hospital did not know exactly what took her from life. I think the shock of her child's death probably caused her also to depart.

My granddaughter passed on October 11, 2003. It was a Saturday. There was a woman Keeper of the Flame in Ghana who was to be married to a Nigerian man on that very day. Her fiancé and his family had come from Nigeria, and they had prepared everything.

I was getting ready to go to our church for the wedding ceremony, where I was to be the presiding minister. Paula's husband came in, tears flowing, crying. He said, "Papa, your grand-daughter has passed on."

Here I was preparing to officiate at a couple's wedding, and here was the news about the passing of my beloved grand-daughter. What was I to do?

I kept this news to myself. I held it in my heart, and I said, "I will not tell any church member about this until I have finished whatever it is that I must do." So apart from my wife and others in the house, I did not tell anybody what had happened.

We went to the wedding, I conducted the ceremony, we held the reception. They even came to my house and had part of the reception there. Nobody in my family showed even a sign that we were in deep mourning.

Sunday, the following day, I was due to fly to Nigeria for an important visit to hold an in-depth study course for the Nigerian students and to conduct some communicant initiations and other sacraments. The question I had was whether to go for these events and rituals or to stay in Accra to take care of the burial of my granddaughter.

She was so close to me, very dear. And yet I had given myself to the Brotherhood, and I had made my pledge that allegiance to them and loyalty to the light was my first priority in this embodiment. So no matter how close I was to my granddaughter, no matter how much I loved her, my duty to the Brotherhood had to come first.

Many years earlier I had told my wife and my mother, "If there is a death in the family and I have an assignment with the church, I will not speak about what happened. I will go and fulfill my assignment. When I have finished and come back, only then I will announce the news to everyone."

So I said to myself, "No, I will not stay in Ghana. I have made my commitment to the Brotherhood, and I will go to Nigeria and fulfill that commitment."* And that was *really* an initiation for me, because it was only with great difficulty that I was able to convince her family on her mother's side that this was my decision and I would not conduct her burial until I had

---

* Jesus demonstrated in his own life that he made his spiritual mission the highest priority, even above commitments to family. At the age of twelve he was found discoursing with the teachers in the temple and told his parents, "wist ye not that I must be about my Father's business?" (Luke 2:48). In the Gospel of Matthew, Jesus exhorted one of his followers to make discipleship a priority over family: "And another of his disciples said unto him, Lord, suffer me first to go and bury my father. But Jesus said unto him, Follow me, and let the dead bury their dead" (8:21–22). Near the beginning of Jesus' public ministry, the Bible records an occasion when his brethren and his mother were calling for him. Mark's Gospel says that Jesus "looked round about on them which sat about him, and said, Behold my mother and my brethren! For whosoever shall do the will of God, the same is my brother, and my sister, and mother" (Mark 3:34–35).

gone to fulfill my assignment from the masters. It was a very severe testing of my commitment, whether I would be faithful to my pledge to the masters even in such a circumstance.

I arranged that the body should be kept at the hospital morgue until we decided when the burial should be. I waited until Wednesday, and then I flew to Lagos for the in-depth study course, the communicant initiations and the other sacraments. After I finished everything at the Lagos group, I flew to Calabar for a seminar there.

It was only then that I told them about the problem I was going through in my family. This was quite a surprise for the people, a marvel. They couldn't believe or understand how I could do that. I told them, "This was a test of my commitment to the Brotherhood, and I cannot fail that test."

It was a very difficult test, a tough initiation for me at that time. I was away for three weeks, all the time with the body of my granddaughter in the mortuary, waiting to be buried.

Perhaps the most painful aspect of this whole experience is that after the sacrifice I had made to be in Lagos for this event, the people there started misbehaving. They came under the influence and manipulation of one of the Keepers of the Flame there, who said that he was the first to join The Summit Lighthouse—which was true, he joined in Ghana before going to Nigeria. He claimed that he was the "father of the teachings" in Nigeria, and that there were certain teachings and things that Mark Prophet told him that even Mother did not know—which of course, was not true.

This man caused a great many problems in the Lagos group. He stirred up the members and the board, and they wrote volumes of letters to headquarters—including complaints about me. Someone at headquarters decided to correspond with them behind my back, and that encouraged them to write even more. It was a very difficult situation, and it continued for some years.

Eventually, the Office of Ministry asked me to go and dismiss the whole board of trustees of the Lagos group, which I did. A new interim board was put in place, and I had to shepherd them, guide them, gradually forming a new board, which is now in charge of the group.

This was also a very hard test for me. I had spent three weeks with them, in spite of the grief that had gripped me with the passing on of my granddaughter, and that was the kind of gratitude that they had showed to me. It was a bitter experience.

However, I learned a great deal. It was not the first time something like this had happened. I had this experience even in the Methodist Church, before I came into these teachings. But it was in working with the Brotherhood that I really learned that if we look for approval from men, we will always be disappointed. If we look for approval from men instead of looking up to our own I AM Presence and the masters, we will always be disappointed.

What comes to my mind when I think of this experience is what the Great Divine Director once said in a dictation. He said that if you are asked to make a pledge and you know that you cannot fulfill that pledge, do not make it. Once you make a pledge, you are held accountable to fulfill that pledge. So it is better not to make a pledge than to make one you know you cannot keep. I have not forgotten this.

Making a pledge is dependent on an individual's perception of what they understand the path to be and their own calling. My advice to anyone is this: If you really want to make your commitment to the Brotherhood, then you really must settle in your heart and mind that you are going to vow to yourself that no matter what happens, you will fulfill whatever you pledge to the masters. You can't make the pledge lightly.

Some may think I am too extreme, but in my heart this is

exactly what I feel, and that is my mind, even now. And that confirms my real commitment to the path and to the Brotherhood, and nothing would make me change it. And what helps me is what the masters by their grace have shown me and my understanding of where I have come from. That is probably what gives me the added conviction about whatever commitment I make. This is the truth in my heart and soul.

Chapter 54

Gold Covering the Earth

I believe that Church Universal and Triumphant is perhaps the only church that can bring true enlightenment to my people, because it is the church that speaks against the ancient vices of witchcraft and black magic, and not only speaks about them but also offers the way out of these practices. This activity is the one that can bring true freedom to the souls of our people.

When I speak to people about our church, I put before them what the church stands for and what the church can do for the souls of the people. As far as I know, there isn't any other church in Africa that has as its priority the deliverance of the soul. They hardly speak about the soul in their preaching, and people ought to be awakened to the existence of the soul and the true meaning of soul freedom.

These great goals can only be achieved through education, enlightening the minds and the hearts of the people. Our people have sunk so low that they need a vision of what they can be. They need to be reminded of the past, of who they are—the blue and the violet race, who lived in a golden age on the continent of Africa, long before recorded history. They must know the glorious past, the spiritual past of the people.* They must know that we have been at the point of a glorious golden age

---

* The history of the ancient golden age and more recent heights of civilization in West Africa is told in Appendix A, "The Destiny of Africa."

before. We are no more at that point because of many different reasons, but there is the possibility that we can get back to that place where we once were. The people must know these things.

Mark Prophet has said, "Ours must be a message of infinite love and we must demonstrate that love to the world." My vision is to see this church rise up and take hold of this mission. It is not just a mission to an individual group of people or any particular nation, but a mission to the whole planet. We realize it must be so when we see that problems affecting one part of the world very easily affect all other parts of the world in these times. Take the problems that affected the nuclear reactors in Japan in 2011. We see that as the wind blows from the west to the east, the radiation is blowing over America and the whole planet. So in thinking of the spiritual rescue of the planet, our thinking must be worldwide and our concerns must be worldwide. That is the vision that I see.

Saint Germain once showed me something about this. I had the opportunity to tell Mother about it when I visited Montana in July 2001. She was retired at that time and living in Bozeman. She was strong in spirit, but not in body, and by this time she could not speak very much.

I met Mother outside a restaurant in Bozeman. When she stepped out of the car, she was so happy to see me, who had come all the way from Africa. She thought she was still strong and she was trying to run, but she could not. Her assistant and I brought her inside and we sat down. I told her of the greatness of this church and the vision that Saint Germain had shown me.

In this vision I found myself in the Middle East, on the coast of Israel bordering on the Mediterranean Sea. Saint Germain dropped a gold piece on the ground, and he said to me, "Pick it up." I tried to pick it up, but it started melting and expanding. This little piece of gold melted and expanded all over the planet. Every island, every continent had a covering of this gold.

I said, "Mother, this vision really strengthened my faith that this teaching will cover the whole planet, every island, everywhere there is land."

Mother said excitedly, "Paul." She was sitting on my right side, slapping my right thigh. And she was trying to find the words—but the words would not come. So she stopped trying to speak.

I spoke with Mother about what this vision meant to me. Saint Germain had showed me the mission and the extent to which this teaching would spread over the planet. We need to wake up and look far afield and find ways of fulfilling this mission for the masters. It is the masters' prophecy and expectation that these teachings should cover the earth, and we can count on them to do their part. But they need us to be the instruments to accomplish this goal.

The masters have their plans. They will supply the materials. But if we don't work with those materials, the expectation cannot be fulfilled. I had to pick up the gold. I could not just stand there and look at it.

It was not just any material that Saint Germain dropped and asked me to pick up. It was gold. I remember Mother has said that she did not understand when Ghanaians said, "We are poor," because in Ghana we are literally sitting and walking on gold. Gold is everywhere in Ghana. There are many gold mines —Ghana used to be called the Gold Coast. In my village, Patriensah, gold is everywhere, but how do we get it up from the soil to the surface? Literally it is everywhere.

Saint Germain said to pick up the gold, and the gold started melting until it covered every square inch on the earth. And that is the destiny of the church. And then I told Mother the final thing that Saint Germain said: "Nothing on earth can prevail against it."

And Mother said, "Yes, that's it!"

Perhaps she wanted to say more, but the masters did not want her to say anything else.

Our challenge in Africa is to launch an onslaught to bring the teachings to the doorstep of everyone on the continent. An onslaught means to bring the teachings to the people by radio, by television, by public outreach. It must not be just an occasional thing. We must have the ability to use the modern means of communication to reach the people. We must use Saint Germain's strategy, his technology, to reach the people. I remember a dictation by the Great Divine Director where he said, "Pursue them. Hold them by the toe. Pull them in." We must use every possible means to bring the people in.

Africa has some very dark history having to do with the fallen ones who settled in Sumer, which is now Iran and Iraq, and came down to South Africa. They worked to tear the people away from their point of first love. They drove a wedge between the people and their God.* We have a bad and fearful history. And there must also be a concerted effort to launch an onslaught for the transmutation of these records. All of this needs planning and drawing up a strategy.

I remember in December 1981, before I went out as the director of the Ghana church, Mother gave instruction to Annice Booth, head of the Office of Ministry, to speak with me. Annice called me to her office and asked me the question, "What are you going to do in Ghana?"

I drew a map of Ghana. Ghana has ten administrative regions, and each region has a capital city. I mapped out these capital cities, and my plan was to ensure that there was a center in each of them. To conquer Africa for the light, we have to do the same thing. We have to map out the countries and develop a plan to reach each of them.

---

* This history is outlined in *The Path of Christ or Antichrist*, by Mark L. Prophet and Elizabeth Clare Prophet, pp. 146–80.

It is not going to be easy in some countries, the ones with rogue governments. Most of the English-speaking countries are fine. But the countries that were associated with European powers other than Britain are difficult to penetrate, because they have security services and secret police that are suspicious about everything. But the effort must be made. We can deal with the easier ones first, and when they are taken care of, then the more difficult ones. We need to muster all the energy to do it, and one necessity will be to hold many decree novenas for these nations.

The possibility of doing all of this is there. Saint Germain's vision of a golden age can become a reality. But the unknown factor in the equation must also be overcome. As Saint Germain says, human beings are unpredictable.

Chapter 55

The Mystery School

Life is a complex adventure. But in the mystery school, it becomes more complex—and even very confusing to the soul. You look at certain situations and you think with the rational mind, "This is the way it should be." But it isn't, and it is difficult to understand why.

In the mystery school, we might think that everyone is toeing the same line. But I think it is a mistake to think that way. We are all in the mystery school as individuals, and as individuals we have our individual burdens and we have our individual freedom. In the past we have used our freedom to act in different ways. Some of our actions have agreed with the law. Others have not. So karma is always a factor, and this is one reason why there are differences in the way we behave towards one another.

You might think that all who come to the mystery school should conform to a certain order. Then we would be sailing smoothly to the goal, but it is not always so. You might think that it should be all joy to help one another to move forward with the mission, but it is not always so. It's mind-boggling when you think of the fact that you have all shades of characters in the mystery school. With my human mind, I would say it should not be so. And yet it has been that way in every mystery school. This is how we receive our initiations and tests on the

269

path.

Jesus told his disciples what would happen after he was gone. He told them they would be persecuted. He told them that the time would come "that whosoever killeth you will think that he doeth God service." He said, "I have told you all this so that when these things should happen, you will remember what I told you." He wanted to equip them to deal with these things. That same message applies to us this day.

When I go through a difficult initiation, I understand that something even bigger and better is ahead. When you get through it, you reach the point where God wanted you to be. Then you can look back at your former self and see how far you have come.

I understand deeply that these initiations are not meant to take us from the path. Rather they are meant to strengthen our resolve and to help us to reach our goal. If you can think of it in this way, you can easily forgive those who have simply become the instruments for the initiation.

Chapter 56

The Guru

My relationship with the Guru was not based on physical proximity. It was an inner relationship. I would say it was a spiritual alliance based on my absolute trust and acceptance of her role as my teacher. I know she understands that level of relationship. And whenever in my ministry I had extreme difficulties or extreme initiations that really taxed my resolve, I would see the Guru in my dreams defending me. She was always with her sword. I remember one incident, which is always before me, the Guru with her sword cutting me free. And then she said, "Paul, you have fought very well."

My mind also goes back often to what Mother told me before I left Camelot in 1981. She said, "Paul, I can see myself always in your house."

Even though it could have been my physical house that she was referring to, since she had been there twice, I also took it to refer to my body temple. That was a good statement. It kept me in trim. It sent my mind back to Romans, chapter 12, when Paul wrote to the church in Rome: "I beseech you therefore, brethren, by the mercies of God, that you present your body a living sacrifice, holy, acceptable unto God, which is your reasonable service." That verse would keep on ringing in my mind.

If the Guru sees herself in my house always, I must strive to make this house habitable. This is not always easy, and living on earth, there will be times I will make mistakes. But even in those difficult times, the Guru will be there to defend me. She is a real Guru who loves her flock.

Now that she has passed, my relationship with her continues. In fact, it is even greater than before, in the sense that now in her new role she has a greater facility of being ever-present. That is what gives me the courage and the joy, in a way, to care less about all the nonsense that others will think they can do to discourage, to prevent, to do something to make me feel disappointed for being on the path. It helps me to look at all of this as the trap of the fallen ones.

My relationship with Mother is a daily one. As my Guru she is always in my mind. And as such I will say my relationship with her is a living relationship, a living and continuous one. Whenever I need any assistance from her, there is an instant recall of her presence. And because she lives daily in my mind, I find it easy to recall the things that she told us. It is especially the things she said concerning me that keep me going—as when she said she would be ever-present to fight my battles for me.

I listen to the other religious spokesmen, the preachers, the pastors, the so-called bishops, I listen to what they say and see how they behave, and I recall my Guru. It amazes me to see the vast difference between a true prophet of God and these ones who are the charlatans, the deceptive ones. Mother was very humble, but very courageous and steadfast, giving out the masters' teaching and defending what she was sent to do.

Elizabeth Clare Prophet is indeed a soul who came out from God. I have learned from her the key to effectively minister unto the people. That key is to love the people, love what you have been entrusted to do. With that key of loving what you have to do, there is no way you cannot succeed. But what I advise myself and the counsel I give to all who have taken the path of service is to not lose sight of the fact that there will always be detractors, people who will seek to take you away from your avowed mission.

Therefore I realize that to be able to stay on course, your resort to the Science of the Spoken Word must never be compromised. Even when you are hard pressed for time or you haven't made the time to go to the altar, let a song be on your lips. You will find me always humming. It is my way of keeping in touch constantly with the masters through decree and prayer.

Mother has been my model. She will continue to be my model until by God's own love and grace we all meet at Luxor, never to return to this earthly life again.

Elizabeth Clare Prophet

The Destiny of Africa

The continent of Africa has a long history. Some of this may be found in history books, but much has been lost to outer memory and may be read only in the records of akasha, which are open to those with spiritual sight.

These records reveal that many thousands of years ago, long before the dawn of recorded history, there was a continent where the Pacific Ocean now is. The people of this continent, which is known as Lemuria, lived in a golden age civilization. Technology, art, science and religion all rose to heights that far exceeded anything since that time on planet Earth.

At the time of Lemuria there was also a golden-age civilization on the continent now known as Africa. The blue race and the violet race lived there at that time, serving on the first ray and the seventh ray. Their descendants live in Africa today as the black race.

Half a million years ago, after the initial fall of man had occurred, the ancient civilization on the continent of Africa had reached a turning point. Because of the fall of man, earth had become vulnerable to the fallen angels—some of them taking embodiment, some of them working on the astral plane to divide the people and enslave them in a cult of darkness. Elizabeth Clare Prophet describes this history:

> These evil angels set out to destroy the blue and the
> violet races. They distorted the once-sacred rituals and

art forms of this people, opening the door to witchcraft, voodoo and black magic. They turned the people toward hatred, superstition a and vying for power.

As the people began to divert their attention from their God Presence, they became more and more vulnerable to the divide-and-conquer tactics of the fallen angels. The civilization became divided by the warring factions of its tribes. The people were losing the inner spiritual battle between the forces of light and darkness within them. And their division, both within and without, allowed them to become enslaved under the powers of darkness.

Seeing the plight of his people, Afra took embodiment among them in order to rescue them. First, he pinpointed the one missing trait that he perceived to be the Achilles' heel of his people. He identified the point of vulnerability as their lack of brotherhood....

Afra knew that many of his people had lost their threefold flame, even as many people, through anger, are losing it today. He also knew that in order to regain that flame, they would have to follow a path of brotherhood. They had to care for one another. The only way he could teach them to be a brother to all others was to be a brother to all himself. And for this, he was crucified by his own people. He was the Christ in their midst, but they knew him not. They were blinded by their greed for power.*

This great one returned to the heart of God in the ritual of the ascension. And thus we know him today as Afra, our brother of light. The ancient golden age of Africa went down, and since that time there has been much darkness on that

---

* *The Masters and Their Retreats,* by Mark L. Prophet and Elizabeth Clare Prophet (Gardiner, Mont.: The Summit Lighthouse Library, 2003), p. 17.

continent. Fallen angels enslaved the people, and the memory of the light that they had once known was lost to outer awareness. One episode of the fallen angels' manipulation of the people is recorded in ancient Sumerian tablets, which tell the story of "Nephilim" and their genetic manipulation of the people, enslaving them to work in their mines in southern Africa.

Yet there have also been eras when a new birth has come forth. Here are a few of the episodes when the light has shone in the continent of Africa.

More than 50,000 years ago, a golden age flourished for a time where the Sahara Desert now is. Sadly, the inhabitants left off the service of the light, and the golden age declined, eventually to be buried under dessert sands.

Thirty-three centuries ago, Ikhnaton and Nefertiti brought forth in Egypt the revelation of Aton, the One God, symbolized in the Sun sending forth its rays of light to all Earth's evolutions. Their reign saw the birth of a new culture of art and beauty unprecedented in the history of their empire, and they established a new religion of brotherhood, love and truth.

Their brief reign came to an end when they were assassinated by Horemheb in a palace coup. Tutankhamen ascended his father's throne at the age of ten, and Horemheb was appointed "lord of the land." The worship of the One God ended and the old gods were brought to supremacy again. Tutankhamen died at the age of eighteen, and soon thereafter Horemheb became pharaoh. Horemheb and his successors sought to erase all record of Ikhnaton and the accomplishments of his reign. His capital city, Amarna, was abandoned, his buildings and temples demolished, and his name erased from monuments. That era was almost lost to history until Amarna was rediscovered and excavated in the nineteenth century.

Four hundred years later, the Queen of Sheba visited King Solomon in Jerusalem. Little is known of her kingdom, and its location is disputed, but the kings of Ethiopia traced their lineage to Makeda, the son of this queen and Solomon himself.

The centuries following Ikhnaton's reign saw increasing challenges for Egypt, both internal and external, with the land coming under the control of a number of foreign powers. In 332 B.C. Alexander the Great conquered Egypt, and his successors set up the Ptolemaic dynasty. They established their capital city at Alexandria, which became the foremost center of learning in the world in the following centuries.

The famed Library of Alexandria was established for the purpose of collecting all of the world's knowledge, and under the Ptolemies and later under Roman rule it grew, according to one account, to more than four hundred thousand volumes, the greatest store of knowledge in the ancient world. We see in this great center of learning the outpicturing of the light of the crown chakra of the continent of Africa (see Appendix E, "The Chakras of Africa"). The great library was burned following the outlawing of Paganism in the Roman Empire in A.D. 391.

In the seventh century A.D. a new Islamic empire spread across North Africa. At the same time a number of new kingdoms arose in sub-Saharan Africa. The Ghana Empire arose in western Africa in what is now Mauritania and Mali. It was known for its wealth in gold, and it reached the height of its power around A.D. 1000, when it rivaled the greatest kingdoms and empires in Europe at that time.

Two hundred years later, remains of the Ghana Empire were incorporated into the Mali Empire, which at its greatest reach extended a thousand miles from modern Mali to the Atlantic. The greatest emperor of Mali, Manca Mussa, astounded the Muslim world when he undertook a pilgrimage to Mecca in 1324 with an entourage of 60,000 and 2,400 pounds of gold to distribute as alms and gifts.

Timbuktu was one of the major cities of the Mali Empire.

Situated on the southern edge of the Sahara Desert, it grew wealthy as a center for trade between Africa and the Mediterranean. The city was also a great center of learning during this period. Sankoré University was the foremost university in the Islamic world, and its fame expanded still further under the Songhai Empire, which succeeded the Mali Empire. The university was capable of housing 25,000 students and it had one of the largest libraries in the world, with between 400,000 and 700,000 manuscripts. Scholars came from North Africa and Europe to confer with the learned historians and writers there.

The greatest ruler of the Songhai Empire was Aksia the Great, who ruled from 1453 to 1538. He expanded the university at Timbuktu and established centers of learning throughout his empire. Scholars and poets from throughout the Muslim world came to his court.

Following the death of Aksia the Great, his empire went into decline. In 1591 the Sultan of Morocco attacked with a large army equipped with European firearms. After standing for five hundred years, the great university at Timbuktu was destroyed and the faculty exiled to Morocco. Attacks from other neighboring lands followed in subsequent centuries, and the great city of Timbuktu, once the queen of the Western Sahara with a population of 200,000, was left with only a shadow of its former glory.

The messenger spoke of this history of past golden ages on the African continent in a lecture in Ghana on September 18, 1978, "Ghana's Destiny in the Holy Spirit." She said that the Empires of Ghana, Mali and Songhai represented the trinity of Father, Son and Holy Spirit. Each brought forth a particular aspect of the consciousness of God. However, after this period, Africa descended into a time of trouble. Internal strife and wars between nations took their toll. With the rise of the age of exploration in Europe, the slave trade flourished. The continent of Africa was divided up and subject to foreign powers for four hundred years.

The dawn of a new era came in 1957, when Ghana became the first African country to attain independence. The independence movements that rose throughout the continent in subsequent decades were a sign that the people sought to break away from the effects of slavery and colonialism and take their place on the world stage.

At the same time as this new light has been rising in Africa, momentums of karma of the past have also been cycling back for transmutation. And the fallen angels and forces of darkness who brought down past golden ages are still entrenched in many places and still seek to hold the people under their subjection. There is a great battle between light and darkness outplaying in Africa, and the outcome will determine the future of a continent and a people who once knew a great light as the blue race and the violet race.

Those who live there today are the descendants of those who built those golden ages that existed in ancient days and during the last two thousand years. The lineage is physical and also spiritual, as people of our day have themselves reembodied from those ancient times. They have the memory of these golden ages that they once knew—and thus of what can rise in that continent in the Aquarian age.

The Ascended Master Afra is the one who sponsors the people of Africa. He spoke to his people when the messenger visited Ghana in 1976. Here is an excerpt of his words:

> I am your brother—not your lord, not your master, but I am your brother on the Path. I have shared your passion for freedom. I have shared with you the hours of crisis when you beheld injustice, when you sought the Lord and prayed to him for justice and the Lord gave to you the divine plan for this nation and for this

continent.

I have lived in your hearts these hundreds and hundreds of years as you have toiled under the burden of oppression from within and without. And although many have considered the outer oppression the greater, we who are among those who have graduated from this continent consider that the only true slavery is the slavery from within—the slavery of the carnal mind and its selfishness, its failure to sacrifice upon the altar as Abraham and Isaac sacrificed. So, the failure to sacrifice the beasts of the carnal mind: this is slavery.

Now then, it is because some have been willing to make the sacrifice of selfishness that the outer slavery has also been broken, and it is the evolution of the people themselves toward the light of God that has given this new opportunity in this age to this continent....

I come, then, that you might see the great flow of the merging of the peoples in the river of the water of life that is the flow of Mother. In the crystal flow of Mother light from the base chakra to the crown of a continent, there is the merging of the people....

Let them leave their nets, let them leave their weapons, let them come at the calling of the Lord and let them hear the call. Let them see the vision, let them have the mind of Afra, let their minds be united in the mandala of a continent. And out of that fiery core of God and of the God design, let them forge first the identity in Christ, then the identity in family, then the identity in community, then the identity in nation, then the identity of a continent.*

---

* Afra, "The Powers and Perils of Nationhood," delivered September 18, 1976, in Accra, Ghana, published in *Afra: Brother of Light,* by Elizabeth Clare Prophet (Gardiner, Mont.: The Summit Lighthouse Library, 2003), pp. 77–78, 79, 81.

Appendix B

The People of Ghana

Ghana is a nation in West Africa, bordered on the west by Côte d'Ivoire (Ivory Coast), on the north by Burkina Faso, on the east by Togo, and on the south by the Gulf of Guinea. It was formerly a British Colony, the Gold Coast, so named for the abundance of gold that is mined there.

In the nineteenth century, most of modern Ghana was part of the Ashanti Empire, one of the most influential states in West Africa in the colonial era. The capital of this empire was Kumasi. Before the city was razed by the British in 1874, the few surviving photographs show a city of unusual beauty, with wide streets lined by houses of a unique architectural style. Nothing of this remains today.

The Ashanti Empire was ruled by a king and a highly-developed system of government with separate ministries to handle the state's affairs and a foreign office to handle relations with foreign powers. The empire was finally conquered by the British in 1894, after a series of wars lasting more than seventy years.

The Ashanti, Kwahu and Fante are three tribes of the Akan people, an ethnic group which makes up about half of the population of Ghana. These tribes speak different dialects of the Akan language, also known as Twi. There are more than one hundred different ethnic groups in Ghana today, including the Ewe (centered in the southeast) and the Ga (found mostly in the area around Accra).

Christianity is the main religion in the south of Ghana and Islam the predominant faith in the north. Christian-Muslim relations in Ghana are peaceful, in contrast to other neighboring countries, such as Nigeria, where sectarian violence is a major concern.

The practice of the traditional fetish religion is also common in Ghana, even among followers of Christianity and Islam. Its followers believe in a supreme god, whose name varies by region, but no priests serve him directly. The priests serve many different spirits and local deities, by whom the priests may be possessed. The presence of spirits of ancestors and the kingdom of the dead are central to the traditional religion, so great importance is placed on the proper conduct of funerals and burial of the dead.

As in most traditional societies, there is a strong extended family system. It is common for poorer members of families to seek financial assistance from relatives who are better off. The strong ties of kinship and the extended family are maintained even among those today who live in modern urban settings or in other countries.

The Akan are a matrilineal society, the family line and inheritance passing through the mother to her children. Polygamy was a common practice in earlier years, especially for wealthy men. A married woman and her children would live with her maternal family. As a result of this, the mother-child bond was stronger than the father-child bond and children were more closely related to their mother's brothers and sisters than to their own fathers. A man's mother, his brothers and sisters, and his maternal nieces and nephews take precedence in inheritance to his own wife and children. These customs have changed in recent years with spread of Christianity and legislation to change the traditional pattern of inheritance.

Appendix C

Decrees for Protection

As you give these decrees to Archangel Michael, visualize this mighty angel arrayed in shining armor and wielding his sword of blue flame. See his presence around you, your family, your friends and all those for whom you are praying. Give the opening prayer or preamble once, repeat the body of the decree three times, nine times, or as many times as you wish, and close with the ending, "And in full faith ..." Use the same pattern for the other decrees included here.

Lord Michael, Cut Me Free!

In the name of the beloved mighty victorious Presence of God, I AM in me, my very own beloved Holy Christ Self, Holy Christ Selves of all mankind, beloved Archangel Michael, beloved Lanello, the entire Spirit of the Great White Brotherhood and the World Mother, elemental life—fire, air, water and earth! I decree:

[Include here calls for specific circumstances or conditions for which you are requesting assistance.]

1. Lord Michael, Lord Michael,
    I call unto thee
   Wield thy sword of blue flame
   And now cut me free!

Refrain: Blaze God-power, protection
   Now into my world,
   Thy banner of faith
   Above me unfurl!

Transcendent blue lightning
   Now flash through my soul,
I AM by God's mercy
   Made radiant and whole!

2. Lord Michael, Lord Michael,
   I love thee, I do
With all thy great faith
   My being imbue!

3. Lord Michael, Lord Michael
   And legions of blue
Come seal me, now keep me
   Faithful and true!

Coda: I AM with thy blue flame
   Now full charged and blest,
I AM now in Michael's
   Blue flame armor dressed! (3x)

And in full faith I consciously accept this manifest, manifest, manifest! (3x) right here and now with full power, eternally sustained, all powerfully active, ever expanding and world enfolding until all are wholly ascended in the Light and free!

Beloved I AM! Beloved I AM! Beloved I AM!

Traveling Protection

Lord Michael before,
Lord Michael behind,
Lord Michael to the right,
Lord Michael to the left,
Lord Michael above,
Lord Michael below,
Lord Michael, Lord Michael wherever I go!

I AM his love protecting here!
I AM his love protecting here!
I AM his love protecting here!

Heart, Head and Hand Decrees
by El Morya

Violet Fire

Heart

    Violet Fire, thou Love divine,
    Blaze within this heart of mine!
    Thou art Mercy forever true,
    Keep me always in tune with you.

Head

    I AM Light, thou Christ in me,
    Set my mind forever free;
    Violet Fire, forever shine
    Deep within this mind of mine.

    God who gives my daily bread,
    With Violet Fire fill my head
    Till thy radiance heavenlike
    Makes my mind a mind of Light.

Hand

    I AM the hand of God in action,
    Gaining Victory every day;
    My pure soul's great satisfaction
    Is to walk the Middle Way.

Tube of Light

Beloved I AM Presence bright,
Round me seal your Tube of Light
From Ascended Master flame
Called forth now in God's own name.
Let it keep my temple free
From all discord sent to me.

I AM calling forth Violet Fire
To blaze and transmute all desire,
Keeping on in Freedom's name
Till I AM one with the Violet Flame.

Forgiveness

I AM Forgiveness acting here,
Casting out all doubt and fear,
Setting men forever free
With wings of cosmic Victory.

I AM calling in full power
For Forgiveness every hour;
To all life in every place
I flood forth forgiving Grace.

Supply

I AM free from fear and doubt,
Casting want and misery out,
Knowing now all good Supply
Ever comes from realms on high.

I AM the hand of God's own Fortune
Flooding forth the treasures of Light,
Now receiving full Abundance
To supply each need of Life.

Perfection

I AM Life of God-Direction,
Blaze thy light of Truth in me.
Focus here all God's Perfection,
From all discord set me free.

Make and keep me anchored ever
In the Justice of thy plan—
I AM the Presence of Perfection
Living the Life of God in man!

Transfiguration

I AM changing all my garments,
Old ones for the bright new day;

With the Sun of Understanding
I AM shining all the way.

I AM Light within, without;
I AM Light is all about.
Fill me, free me, glorify me!
Seal me, heal me, purify me!
Until transfigured they describe me:
I AM shining like the Son,
I AM shining like the Sun!

Resurrection

I AM the Flame of Resurrection
Blazing God's pure Light through me.
Now I AM raising every atom,
From every shadow I AM free.

I AM the Light of God's full Presence,
I AM living ever free.
Now the flame of Life eternal
Rises up to Victory.

Ascension

I AM Ascension Light,
Victory flowing free,
All of Good won at last
For all eternity.

I AM Light, all weights are gone.
Into the air I raise;
To all I pour with full God Power
My wondrous song of praise.

All hail! I AM the living Christ,
The ever-loving One.
Ascended now with full God Power,
I AM a blazing Sun!

Reverse the Tide

In the name of the beloved mighty victorious Presence of God, I AM in me, my own beloved Holy Christ Self and Holy Christ Selves of all mankind, beloved Cyclopea, thou Silent Watcher for the earth, beloved seven mighty Elohim, beloved seven Chohans and Archangels, beloved Mighty Astrea, beloved Lanello, the entire Spirit of the Great White Brotherhood and the World Mother, elemental life—fire, air, water and earth! I decree:

TAKE DOMINION NOW OVER:
[Give the following insert or compose your own prayer for the specific situation you are working on.]
All black magic, witchcraft, prayers of malintent, hatred, anger or condemnation directed against me, my family, my livelihood, or my service to life.

> * Reverse the tide! (3x)
> Roll them back! (3x)
> Reverse the tide! (3x)
> Take thy command!
> Roll them back! (3x)
> Set all free! (3x)
> Reverse the tide! (3x)
> (*Repeat this section 3, 12, or 36 times.)

Replace it all by the glorious principles of God-freedom, of cosmic liberty for the expansion of the Christ flame in every heart and for the mighty plan of freedom for this age from the heart of beloved Saint Germain!

> Unite the people in liberty! (3x)
> By God's own love now set them free! (3x)
> Unite the earth and keep it free (3x)
> By each one's I AM victory! (3x)
> Expose the Truth! (12x)
> Expose the lie! (12x)

And in full faith ...

Decree to Beloved Mighty Astrea

In the name of the beloved mighty victorious Presence of God, I AM in me, mighty I AM Presence and Holy Christ Selves of Keepers of the Flame, Lightbearers of the world and all who are to ascend in this life, by and through the magnetic power of the sacred fire vested in the threefold flame burning within my heart, I call to beloved Mighty Astrea and Purity, Archangel Gabriel and Hope, beloved Serapis Bey and the Seraphim and Cherubim of God, beloved Lanello, the entire Spirit of the Great White Brotherhood and the World Mother, elemental life—fire, air, water and earth! to lock your cosmic circles and swords of blue flame in, through, and around my four lower bodies, my electronic belt, my heart chakra and all of my chakras, my entire consciousness, being, and world.

[Include here calls for specific circumstances or conditions for which you are requesting assistance.]

Cut me loose and set me free (3x) from all that is less than God's perfection and my own divine plan fulfilled.

1. O beloved Astrea, may God Purity
   Manifest here for all to see,
   God's divine will shining through
   Circle and sword of brightest blue.

First chorus: Come now answer this my call
   Lock thy circle round us all.
   Circle and sword of brightest blue,
   Blaze now, raise now, shine right through!

2. Cutting life free from patterns unwise,
   Burdens fall off while souls arise
   Into thine arms of infinite love,
   Merciful shining from heaven above.

3. Circle and sword of Astrea now shine,
   Blazing blue white my being refine,

Stripping away all doubt and fear,
Faith and goodwill patterns appear.

Second chorus: Come now answer this my call,
Lock thy circle round us all.
Circle and sword of brightest blue,
Raise our youth now, blaze right through!

Third chorus: Come now answer this my call,
Lock thy circle round us all.
Circle and sword of brightest blue,
Raise mankind now, shine right through!

And in full faith ...

Give each verse followed by the first chorus; repeat the verses using the second chorus; then give the verses a third time using the third chorus.

I AM the Violet Flame

In the name of the beloved mighty victorious Presence of God, I AM in me, my very own beloved Holy Christ Self, and Holy Christ Selves of all mankind, I decree:

I AM the violet flame
In action in me now
I AM the violet flame
To light alone I bow
I AM the violet flame
In mighty cosmic power
I AM the light of God
Shining every hour
I AM the violet flame
Blazing like a sun
I AM God's sacred power
Freeing every one

And in full faith ...

Appendix D

A Brief History of
The Summit Lighthouse
in Ghana

Excerpted from the Thirty-Third Anniversary
Commemorative Journal of the Church Universal and
Triumphant of Ghana, 1998

The Summit Lighthouse was founded on August 7, 1958, in Washington, D.C., by Mark L. Prophet under the direction of the Ascended Master El Morya, Chief of the Darjeeling Council of the Great White Brotherhood.

In the early sixties, vibrations of the ascended masters' activity had reached Ghana and one or two individuals had started corresponding with it. One such individual was the late Alexander Krakue, who by the end of 1964 had registered as a Keeper of the Flame. The earliest correspondence in our files was addressed to Mr. K. E. Donkoh, dated November 1964.

On March 20, 1965, Alexander Krakue formed a Study Group of The Summit Lighthouse in Accra by registering six additional students with the headquarters in U.S.A.

Initially, the meeting place was at Mataheko, Accra, the residence of Alexander Krakue. When old Alex moved to Tema, a brother by the name of Mr. Kofi Darko offered his home at Ridge for the meetings. When this brother was posted outside Ghana, the meeting place moved to Mamprobi, to the residence of Mr. Herbert Krakue, who later became Bishop of the Church.

To operate within the legal framework of Ghana the activity was registered with the Deeds Registry as The Summit Lighthouse Church on July 29, 1967. At this point the headquarters referred to us as "The First Summit Lighthouse Church." As the membership grew a house was rented at Kanda in Accra in 1968 to serve as the sanctuary.

In 1972, by the command of the Darjeeling Council, Mark and Elizabeth Prophet paid their first visit to Ghana. During their visit they delivered the Teachings of the Ascended Masters at the First African Summit Conference. It was held in the Commonwealth Hall Chapel, University of Ghana, from July 21 to 23. About seventy members and aspirants were in attendance.

The conference program included a welcome address, decrees, prayers, songs, meditations, baptisms, teachings on the cosmic history of Africa and the blue and violet races, and on Ghana as the focus of Saint Germain and Portia (symbolized in Ghana's motto, "Freedom and Justice"). At the baptism ceremony, one member chose the baptismal name of Sanat Kumara, and upon Mark mentioning this name, the bowl of water and rose petals used for the baptism began to shake.

In all, ten lectures and seven dictations were given. To crown all these visible and describable activities there was an invisible and indescribable impartation and communion of heart which participants experienced as a group and as individuals, each according to his or her level of attainment and attunement.

The messengers stayed at a guest house at the University of Ghana, Legon, courtesy of the then registrar, Dr. E. A. K. Edzii. Dr. Edzii was not formerly a member, but came forward to be baptized during the conference. (Dr. Edzii became Executive Secretary of the Board in 1996.)

Prior to the conference, the messengers visited many places around Accra. They also cruised on Volta Lake, where they established a focus to connect with the resurrection flame at the headquarters of the activity in Colorado Springs, which flame the Messengers carried to Egypt and the Great Pyramid in September 1972, thus giving impetus to the approaching millennium. A flame of Buddhic consciousness was also established on the University of Ghana campus.

The first visit of the messengers was an Alpha thrust in the history of the Church in Ghana and a turning point of spiritual significance for Africa. Ghana is the heart chakra of Africa, and Africa houses the Great Pyramid, which is the storehouse of the destiny of planet earth—past, present and future. Man's journey upon earth ends in Africa at the Ascension Temple over Luxor, Egypt.

The Messengers, in a letter of gratitude to the church dated August 22, 1972, said, "We know that because you have chosen to rise, millions of Africans will also choose to rise with you. And we know that the spiral that was begun at Legon shall continue to rise in thirty-three tiers until the pyramid of Light is complete, the capstone is in place, and Africa as a continent ascends to the level of God-awareness."

In following years, the Church continued to grow from strength to strength spiritually, materially and in membership. By the end of 1973 the impact of the Church had been felt throughout Ghana, manifesting in the opening of centers in Kumasi, Takoradi and Dunkwa-on-Offin in addition to Accra.

In 1973 the landlady of the sanctuary at Kanda requested her property and consequently the Church moved from Kanda to Odorkor on December 31, 1973, to a property of the father-in-law of the then Director, Rev. Herbert H. Krakue. Efforts were immediately made to secure a suitable piece of land for the Church, but as this was delayed the Director offered a piece of land adjoining the temporary sanctuary at Odorkor for the construction of a permanent sanctuary.

The construction was started and completed with lightning speed. By the next visit of the Messenger Elizabeth Clare Prophet in September 1976 (Mark having ascended on February

26, 1973) the sanctuary was ready for dedication. On the day of dedication, under the direction of Ascended Master El Morya, the messenger consecrated the then Director as the Bishop of Africa with the responsibility of spreading the Teachings of the Ascended Masters in Ghana and the whole of Africa. At the time this was the only bishopric in the church worldwide, and this office also emphasized Ghana's responsibility of spreading the Teachings of the Ascended Masters in the whole of Africa.

During the 1976 visit of the messenger, the Second Africa Summit Lighthouse Conference was organized. It took place in the auditorium of the School of Administration, University of Ghana, Legon, from September 16 to 19, 1976. An important feature of this visit was the ordination of nine lay ministers (eight for Ghana and one for Nigeria) and three apostles (two for Ghana and one for Nigeria) charged to spearhead the expansion program of the activity in Africa.

In January 1978, the Ghana Church had the rare opportunity of being host to the messenger for the third time. On that occasion, the mother church redesignated The Summit Lighthouse Church in Ghana as Church Universal and Triumphant of Ghana under a new constitution dated January 18, 1978, and duly registered with the government of Ghana on September 7, 1978. The purpose of this third visit, among other things, was to share her ideas with Ghanaians on the concept of Union Government, which the government of the time was placing before Ghanaians in a referendum.

The messenger gave a series of lectures in which she explained the concept of God-government. Her exposé was based on the premise that the future government that Ghanaians were laboring to have should be founded upon the shoulders of the "Christed One" prophesied in Isaiah 9:16.

By 1980, two major centers had been opened at Akim Oda, and Nkawkaw, bringing the total of centers in Ghana to six. However, 1980 was a year of fundamental change, an end to the first dispensation under the Blue Flame of the Father. The Bishop lost his leadership position and the Church also lost its Odorkor sanctuary, as there were no legal documents to establish its bona fide ownership by the church. This was a period of great pain and initiation for the entire membership.

The headquarters appointed an Interim Committee to run the affairs of the Church. Through the assistance of some dedicated members, the Church, by the end of 1981, had access to an abandoned club house in South Legon which was converted into a sanctuary.

In 1982, Rev. Paul K. Kyei was appointed the director of the Church for its second life cycle. Under a second ray dispensation, he pursued a vigorous expansion program through outreach. The Church was represented on Ghana TV programs *Contemplation* and *About Life*. The tangible result of the expansion program was the opening of new centers in the following towns and communities: Koforidua, Apirede (Akuapem), Leklebi/Hohoe, Keta, Ho, Obuasi, Axim/Ahanta, University of Science and Technology (Kumasi) and Tamale.

Between 1984 and 1985, the accommodation problem arose again. The residents of South Legon demanded the release of the sanctuary to be used once again as club house. At this critical moment Mrs. Sybil Foli willingly offered her house at Abelemkpe to be used temporarily as a sanctuary. The Church moved into this house on March 2, 1986.

Ghana's role in giving ministerial support to Nigeria continued during the term of office of Rev. Kyei. Visits were made not only to Lagos but also to other centers in western and eastern Nigeria, whilst Rev. Kobina E. Donkoh, who was then resident in Kaduna, took charge of the north.

In December 1995, the term of Rev. Kyei came to an end. This was in line with headquarters' new policy of giving opportunity to different people to serve in the highest office of the Church. The headquarters expressed "sincere appreciation for his many years of dedicated and selfless service as President of the Ghana Church, who steadfastly held the flame in Ghana."

Rev. Donkoh, a founding member of the Church, was appointed the new director for a third life cycle, from January 1996. Under a third ray dispensation of divine love of the Holy Spirit, he preaches the empowerment of the Holy Spirit through the application of the ascended masters' teachings.

In July 1996, at long last, the church commenced construction of a permanent church complex. The ground floor was dedicated on March 22, 1998, at the 33rd Anniversary celebration of the founding of The Summit Lighthouse in Ghana. It must be stated that the impetus for the building project was the offer of a more suitable plot of land by a member. The zeal of the general membership (both local and abroad), in building fund contributions, tithes and special offerings, backed with supply novenas, precipitated the alchemy with the blessing of the masters, for which we are grateful.

THE FUTURE

"May each one ponder the dilemma of his future. Go to the heart of Sanat Kumara, Lord Gautama and Lord Jesus Christ to make your peace, through the law of forgiveness, with all whom you have wronged. This do, beloved, and know your freedom day by day." —Afra, April 4, 1997

We see:

A future where our church complex shall be complete, with a magnificent chapel with the motif of a Lighthouse.

A future where the Teachings of the Ascended Masters are taken to each home through the mass media—newspapers, radio and television.

A future where "Africa, as a continent, ascends to the level of God-awareness." —the Messengers

SO BE IT, IN GOD'S HOLY NAME, I AM

The Chakras of Africa

A chakra is a spiritual center or energy field for the release of light and energy to the body of man. Just as the human body has seven major chakras, so a nation or a continent also has forcefields of energy that correspond to the seven chakras, and these release light and energy to the rest of the nation or continent. The chakras of any nation can give insight into the kinds of negative energies or problems that exist in an area and also indicate the strengths and divine purpose intended to manifest there.

Elizabeth Clare Prophet has outlined the chakras of the continent of Africa as bands of latitude, from the base-of-the-spine chakra in the south to the crown chakra in the north. The map on the next page shows the approximate location of the chakras based on her descriptions.

The energy of the base chakra is seen in South Africa in the vast mineral wealth that is found there and in the white light of the Mother focused in the retreat of the Goddess of Purity over the island of Madagascar.

The retreat of Arcturus and Victoria, Elohim of the seventh ray, is at Luanda, Angola, at the level of the seventh-ray chakra, the seat of the soul.

The level of the solar plexus includes Congo, Uganda and Rwanda, nations that have seen great misuse of this energy in civil war and genocide.

The heart chakra includes Ghana, Nigeria and other nations that are home to souls with great heart quality and a destiny to expand the light of the heart and the threefold flame.

The level of the throat and third-eye chakras includes the Sahara Desert and nations to its south. It was the misuse of the energies of these chakras in black magic and witchcraft that was used to bring down the ancient golden age of the blue and violet races on the continent of Africa. The karmic return for this misuse is seen in the barrenness of these areas and the periodic famines that devastate these nations.

The crown chakra is the most northern part of the continent, including northern Egypt, the Sinai Peninsula, the Holy Land and the Fertile Crescent. The crown chakra is where the light of God as Father is anchored in the body of man, and these lands saw the birth of religions that were intended to release the understanding of God as Father and Divine Law—Judaism, Christianity, Islam and the original revelation of the one God through Ikhnaton.

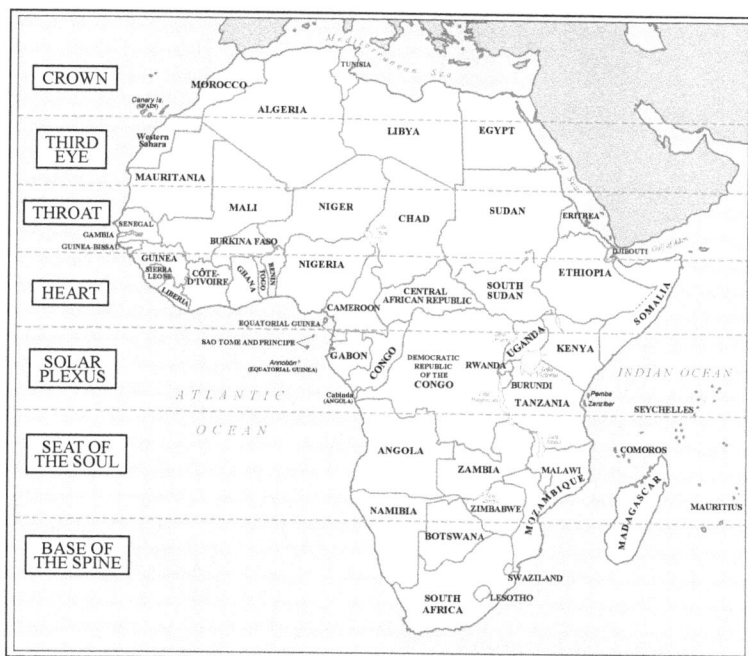

www.ingramcontent.com/pod-product-compliance
Lightning Source LLC
Chambersburg PA
CBHW022116080426
42734CB00006B/149